My Mother Wore a
Yellow Dress

CHRISTINA McKENNA

Neil Wilson Publishing, Glasgow

First published by
Neil Wilson Publishing Ltd
303 The Pentagon Centre
36 Washington Street
GLASGOW
G3 8AZ

Tel: 0141-221-1117
Fax: 0141-221-5363
E-mail: info@nwp.co.uk
www.nwp.co.uk

ISBN 1-903238-76-5
Typeset in Mrs Eaves
Printed in Poland

For my mother,
Mary McKenna née Henry,
in memoriam,

and
Mr Kiely

This existence of ours is as transient as autumn clouds. To watch the birth and death of beings is like looking at the movements of a dance. A lifetime is like a flash of lightning in the sky, rushing by like a torrent down a steep mountain.

Gautama Buddha

Contents

Acknowledgements

The following are poems quoted in the text.

The quote on page 216 is from Edmund Spenser (1552-99); that on page 233 is from Anthony Robbins (1960-); the final quote on page 245 is taken from *Salut au Monde* by Walt Whitman (1819-92).

A Glossary of Ulster Scots

at the back of	the cause of
bate	to beat
bee t' be	must have been
blade	a quick-witted woman
blether	to talk nonsense
boys a dear	Is that so?/You don't say!
brae	a hill-slope
carnaptious	grumpy, irritable
ceilidh	a visit, to visit
clatt	a dirty or untidy person
craic	lively conversation
cretur	an unfortunate
dander	to stroll
declerta	I declare to [God]
dizzier	a local female character
drig	to drink greedily
footer	to potter, to work in a time-wasting way
gulpen	a stupid person
gype	a fool or clown
hoke	to forage, rummage
keep fut till	to keep up with
larnin	learning
lock	a small quantity/a few
make a shape	to woo/make a move
mine	to remember
nearderhan	nearer
pallions	unnecessary clothing
plunther	to plod, trudge

puke	an unfriendly or proud person
quare	very, considerable, strange
quet	to stop
rickle	an unstable object
rig-out	an outfit [of clothing]
sappy	sorry, unfortunate
schaghey	an odd mixture of food
sheugh	a drain or ditch
slooter	a sloppy person
spraghal	to walk awkwardly
stotious	drunk
taig	a Catholic
tarra	terrible
tekelin	a very old vehicle
thole	to put up with, endure
throughother	all mixed up, disorderly
tight	smart, sharp, brave
too much ground	extravagant
trig	neat, smartly dressed
wan	one
wain	a baby
wheen	a few
whitred	a weasel
wile	terrible, very

PROLOGUE

I learned about conflict from my parents. My mother used words as weapons; my father used the angered silence. Within the confines of this senseless arrangement they produced nine of us and gave rise to the fear and insecurity that would dominate most of our lives.

My parents are dead now: all that furious, unfocused energy gone – stilled together in the grave. They surely rest in peace. My mother was in need of a concentrated dose of it. But the anger and resentment and the thwarted logic that fund such emotions is apparent from time to time in my siblings and me; such is the legacy we have been left to grapple with.

This is the story of my journey out of a lonely childhood into the dissonant world of the adult. It's about the mother who cared for me and tried to smooth the way, and the father who couldn't, who charged on ahead regardless, letting the briars and branches of his discontent crash into me, to cause me to stumble, to defeat me and make me bleed.

It's about a few good people who loved me and urged me on. It's about the many who could not love themselves and so held me back, wrecking the pure and present oneness of what I tried to be.

Throughout the journey there was God, bending to fit the cliché of what others said He was. It took a supernatural event in our home in 1970 to confirm for me the existence of this supreme being. It would also trigger in me the need to question the reality of things rather than blindly accept everything 'as is'. Finding the truth beneath all the limiting belief systems I grew up with then became my quest.

That search is not an easy one. The fearful past strives to keep me bound, while my higher self calls to set me free. I realise, however, that understanding the people and events of those earlier years, rather than blaming them, is what leads to peace and draws me closer to that truth or the divine spark that lies within all of us. Following this path is a life's work. It involves the continuing education of my heart and soul.

Honeymoon

They were married in April 1946. The wedding photo shows a striking pair. My mother was beauty itself: pale complexion, lovely cobalt eyes and luxuriant, wavy hair that would stay stubbornly black till the day she died. In the picture she stands beside the seated figure of my father. His face is stern and handsome, hers wears a tranquil and knowing smile. This arrangement would be emblematic of their lives together: my mother always on her feet, the worker bee; my father forever the seated, sedentary drone.

Who knows what was going through their heads as they gazed into the lens and out towards their unresolved futures? I sense little affection in this image. They do not link arms or hold hands. They inhabit separate worlds. This then is not a marriage of passion but of need.

The camera shutter shuffles and clicks several times in Keogh Photography Studios off St Stephen's Green. The scene is frozen and framed. They walk out into the bustle of Dublin city in their stiff new clothes and so their married life begins.

After the muted ambience of the studio the city startles anew. The brightness, the noise, and the leaden air. There is a clash of colours and smells: a mix of burnt hops from Guinness's Brewery, the putrid yellowing of a smoke-filled sky and the stench of the Liffey. This stench is the worst. My mother feels unwell and my father is anxious. He rushes ahead of her down Grafton Street. He does not think to take her hand or ask how she is and, if he does, feels too awkward to put deed to thought. She has difficulty keeping up and collides with a cyclist, making him swear and swerve. Her new shoes show little sympathy for her feet.

She knows that her husband is looking for his older brother Robert, who has been waiting outside Brown Thomas for the photo session to finish. Robert has accompanied them on their honeymoon because he's familiar with the city. My parents have never been to their nearest city Belfast, let alone Dublin. They're like lost children in a maze and are glad of Robert's guiding hand.

When they finally see him amid the crowd they both breathe a sigh of relief. He is easy to spot because he cuts an impressive figure; with his trilby, belted gabardine coat and serious air he resembles a spy left over from the war.

Robert acknowledges the pair with a brief nod and strides ahead. No words are spoken and they are grateful to see that he's heading into Bewley's Oriental Café. Once inside, they form a clumsy trio round a table, and after much hesitation order a cream tea. The air quivers between them. They feel this new experience as a panic rising in them, making the hands unsteady, the words unsure. While all about them conversations ebb and flow, laughter rolls and ripples, fragile cups are raised and lowered, forks sink through pastry, making the china clink and ring. A whole symphony of sound and movement unfolds around them and they feel excluded, ill at ease in the carefree élan of the gathering.

Mother eases off her shoes and sighs. She reaches for a cake and is suddenly conscious of her red, coarsened hands. She's 27 and has been a workhorse for most of those years. She coughs to cover her embarrassment and looks forward to a better life – a life that will not include the endless scrubbing of shirttails and collars, the drudgery of keeping five brothers presentable. They'll just have to find someone else to skivvy for them, and her mother will have to find someone else to bully.

With this thought a light snaps on in a new world, lighting up the house that she has planned; a home of her own at last. She imagines moving through its coloured landscape, making the contours of it fit the shape of things to come. She sees the sky leaning in at spotless windowpanes, sun-plated surfaces that shine, a washed floor drying without trespass, floral curtains, scented rooms, potted plants on sills.

She longs for the space that was pulled from her as she grew up and sees it now unfurling in the parlour she will sit in, the garden she'll look out on. The urge to stay in this other world is strong; she lets her thoughts roam through the quiet spaces of her dream house, not wanting to return to the noise and bustle of the café.

But return she does, grafting her dream onto the man at her side, her newly acquired husband. She looks at him now and all he offered her: a handsome face, a promise of money, a gold wedding band and – perhaps most important of all – a ready escape.

> So for your face I have exchanged all faces,
> For your few properties bargained the brisk
> Baggage, the mask-and-magic-man's-regalia.

She allows herself a rueful smile and looks out of the café window, to the trams and carts of the homeward bound – a film with the sound turned down.

Spent cigarettes still fume in the ashtray. The brothers are talking but have made no attempt to include her; a river of words running past her, leaving her stranded. A woman is a foreigner in their company. It is hot and humid in the café and cigarette smoke hangs like a great amorphous witness over the three of them. Robert steals covert glances at the bride's perfect profile and marvels at her beauty. He regrets that he couldn't have made a shape himself and resents his brother for having achieved the elevated status of the married man. After all he, Robert, is a man of letters, has been out in the world; educated at college in London – qualified with honours – and is blessed with all the concomitant aspirations and awareness that go with these things. A flame of resentment flares up in him now, a flame that will flicker and burn in him for the rest of his days. He tries now to contemplate the implications of the married state, but his mind contracts. He cannot, or rather will not, envisage such intimacy and suddenly cancels the reverie with a comment.

'Grand place this, asay.' He gazes up at the ceiling as he speaks.

But father isn't listening. He's parted one of the sandwiches and is examining the contents.

'What sorta schaghey's that?' he asks.

Mother, being a woman, feels moved to respond to this culinary query.

'It's salad. Y'know: lettuce and tomato and stuff … ' she trails off uneasily.

'I don't care what it is!' the bridegroom snaps. 'Wouldn't fill a bloody rabbit, let alone a man.'

He closes the sandwich, returns it to the plate, and selects another for examination. Robert can no longer ignore his brother's crude antics and glares at him.

'Are ye gonna do that with evirything on the plate, are ye? We have to ate too, y'know. Could ye not conduct yirself when yir outtamong the people?'

'Sappy lotta people,' says father, looking around. 'Pack of oul' pukes. And thir's no need for you to be gettin' so carnaptious.'

He wolfs the sandwich and takes a noisy slurp of the tea. Several patrons cast glances at their table. Mother, somewhat embarrassed and sensing a dispute between the brothers, rushes in to keep the peace.

'It doesn't matter, Robert,' she says. 'I'm finished anyway.'

Father, to the relief of all concerned, decides that he too has eaten enough, and throws back his head to drain the dregs in the teacup. He puts it down with a clatter on the saucer and announces, 'Quare tay that … better than that bloody British dishwater you get up in the North. They know how to do things in the Free State, I'm tellin' ye.'

He now turns in his seat to have a good gape around. He will never be one to observe the refinement and dignity certain situations demand, being more prone to the cock-up and the clanger. His discourtesy invites some strange looks but he assumes not to notice. 'Not used out, just up for the day' is probably the consensus that ripples through the onlookers.

Father's hobby is carpentry and when it comes to furniture he shows an obsessive interest in how things are put together. He now thumps the back of the chair, gives it a right good shake and announces to the gathering that it's about an inch off true and made of plywood – 'only oul' rubbish.'

A waiter hovers nervously, faces strain with astonishment; a tide of pink creeps up my mother's neck. She's shocked, but sooner rather than later will have to get used to her husband's idiosyncrasies. Robert goes looking for the toilet.

My father's forensic interest in joinery and his habit of attacking unsuspecting pieces of furniture in public will not diminish with the years. Once, while staying in a B&B in Donegal, my sister and I were summoned from our bedroom by an almighty thundering on the stairs. We found him hammering away on the banister, testing the firmness of its anchorage. He concluded aloud that it was only 'an oul' rickle', oblivious to the fact that the lady of the house had appeared behind him in a speechless state, clutching at her nightdress and on the verge of collapse. No doubt she'd thought she was being burgled – or worse. We mumbled our apologies, backed father into his room and took the precaution of locking him in.

But that was later.

For now, for my mother, these things are a portent of what is to come. She is aware of a chink in the armour of her chosen prince. She wonders at this coarse betrayal – that inconsiderate display. Robert, ever the schoolmaster, sees her distress and takes control. He beckons the waiter with a nod and very soon they are out of there.

Robert now realises that his brother cannot be trusted in reputable establishments, and swiftly aborts a plan for alcoholic refreshment at the Gresham Hotel. Something needs to be done, he thinks, and duly adjusts his itinerary. So he forgoes the genteel tea shops and hotels in favour of the less salubrious cafés and much frequented hostelries. There are many pubs in Dublin and he now heads for the dingiest one he can think of: The Mizzen Mast, near Amiens Street train station.

Robert finds its atmosphere ideal: a nexus of Mickies and Paddies from the mountains and bogs, with their flat caps, stubble and toothless talk. Once inside, the schoolmaster can relax, content in the knowledge that his brother will blend seamlessly with this rough assemblage. His sister-in-law is not so content; what with her new pink suit and newly acquired airs, she certainly has no wish to spend time in this dive. But on an intellectual level she understands the logic of Robert's choice. The men drink whiskey, the lady a sweet sherry. The bridegroom drinks for courage and Robert drinks to forget. And the bride, well, she drinks for luck. She really feels she's going to need it.

One year later my mother was pregnant with her first child. She would give birth to nine more, her once youthful body collapsing and thickening under the strain. I came in as number seven. My youngest brother was born in 1963, and we as a family were complete.

Lessons in Heaven

Which of us can bear witness to their earliest years? As I roll out the map of my life and look at that used-up part of it, viewing my past through the present, one region remains tightly closed, unable to surrender its mysteries and proceedings: my infancy.

My mother told me that my birth had been easy, and that the tiles had slid off the roof in the 80-degree heat of that midsummer's day. She neglected to tell me, however, that 1957 witnessed more notable events. The Russians sent the first dog into space on Sputnik 2 and women were admitted to the House of Lords for the first time. I doubt if these milestones impacted in any way on her busy life.

My life only begins to assume definition and colour for me when I turn four. I am standing on the kitchen floor, looking up at three pictures on a wall: the Sacred Heart with its burning candle and a portrait on either side: those of President John F Kennedy and Pope John XXIII. My mother is tying my shoelaces. I sense her unhappiness. She shouts at my brother Mark to hurry up with his porridge. She admonishes my older sister Rosaleen for not having her hair combed. My baby brother John screams in his cot.

I stand there silent and scared amid the mayhem. I hear mother's voice rise by turns with annoyance and fall to a whisper in my ear.

'You're going to love school,' she tells me.

But I am not convinced. I do not understand what 'school' means. What I do know and experience for the first time is fear: fear of leaving home and fear of leaving *her*.

When I see her produce a small cardboard suitcase with brass corners I sense danger and my pulse quickens. Inside it she puts a pencil, a jotter and a Paris bun wrapped in loaf paper. She then takes my hand and, with my brother and sister in tow, we set out for school.

I am escorted unwillingly through that still September morning. The sun stretches across the flat fields and roaming hedges. I gaze at the ragwort that abounds left and right; it slows with my reluctance and speeds up with my mother's impatience as she tugs me along. The trees whisper above me as I walk.

Calmly a cloud stands, calmly a bird sings

Crossing the Forgetown bridge I hear the river clattering over the stones. These are the sounds and scenes I'd come to know so well.

In my childhood trees were green
And there was plenty to be seen.

As our destination draws closer I struggle to keep my tears at bay. My fear and bewilderment increase.

Letting go of my hand at the end of that journey is a significant betrayal on my mother's part. I tighten my fist round the hook of her thumb and bawl and wail. My tears are hot and blinding. My heart hammering at the infamy of such a desertion.

It is not an abandonment, I soon learn, but a handing over into the care of an angel: my new teacher. Miss McKeague strokes my hand with a gentle 'Now, now, dear', and so eases my passage from one blurry world into another. ...

Lisnamuck Primary, some three miles from the town of Maghera, was housed in the typical rural school building of the time. It was a simple, two-roomed structure built on a slight incline, whitewashed and drably lifted with a coat of fading blue on windows and doors. A low wall and gate shielded us from the roadway. To one side was a playing field where we were let loose at lunchtime for that necessary respite from the daily grind.

In Miss's room there were four rows of miniature desks and chairs, each row representing a year-group from P1 to P4. As each year passed I would be informed and altered, progressing from row to row, from start to finish, from the front to the back of the room.

The most prominent feature was a large fat-bellied stove, kept burning all winter. There was an ominous guardrail around it which warned us of its danger and kept our childish inquisitiveness in check. The blackboard stood to the right of the fire and faced us accusingly. The only remaining items of furniture were Miss's desk and several cupboards, bloated with layers of shiny, pink paint. The cupboards contained the tricks of her trade, for our instruction and play. There were books and pencils, paint sets and brushes, toys and skipping ropes. All this equipment would help me engage with a whole new world and tease my brain down new pathways of learning.

Miss McKeague was the enchantress who would make this paraphernalia live. She was the omniscient presence that would keep an attentive vigil for the next four years and represent all a child desired from a teacher and adult: calmness, stability, gentleness and grace.

Looking back now I can see that she was a cliché of her time — a model of rectitude and fine breeding, with that dedication to duty that only the selfless spinster can lay claim to. She was the quintessential teacher, who had flattened all her ambitions to fit the classroom — in a drift of ruled lines, squeaking chalk and red comments in margins.

There was nothing fussy or complicated about her. She wore serviceable tweed suits in blue or grey, and dependable low-heeled shoes in black or brown. Her silver hair was always gathered into a bun. Often some strands would slip their moorings to frame her kindly, unpainted face and watchful, sympathetic eyes. Those eyes were her finest, most distinctive feature. Her only artificial adornments were a pearl brooch and a simple watch that served the dual purpose of telling the time and securing a forever pristine handkerchief at her wrist.

There was little deviation from routine with Miss. We lined up every morning to await her ever-punctual arrival. She would park her Hillman Minx in the same careful spot by the school gate, then crunch down the hill with her little tan suitcase and her smile. Her singsong greeting seldom varied and we'd respond in kind.

'Good morning, children.'

'Good morning, Miss McKeague.'

'Very cold this morning, children, isn't it?'

'Yes, Miss McKeague.'

She would then appoint someone to hold the case while she fished for the keys. Offering up our little arms as supports, we all jostled for this privilege. But we needn't have: everyone got their turn in due course. Once she'd found the key she'd turn it in the lock, yank open the swollen door, causing the tongued latch to rattle its objection. We would file in obediently, shrug off our coats, and so our day would begin.

I was never at ease in school and not even Miss's love could change this. I looked at others with fear and longing: those girls with bouncy ringlets and shiny shoes who could talk and laugh easily and got all the answers right. By comparison I was not a pretty child – or should I say that little attempt was made to prettify me? I was the seventh child born to a harassed mother, and I can well understand that she had probably given up caring too much at that stage. My little podgy face was marred by a pair of round pink spectacles and a blunt, chin-length haircut, that looked as though mother had used a pair of hedge clippers. She topped off the look with a white ribbon, tied in an enormous bow. The bow seemed like a rueful afterthought, some kind of vain attempt at glamorising the dull little package that was me.

Gradually, in the warm presence of my new temporary mother, I began to thaw and hesitantly unfold my wings, stretching them out to the sides of my desk to touch my equally tremulous classmates. I sat beside Doreen and made tentative friends with her. She broke into my solitude and gave me the acceptance I needed in the vast, strange world of school.

Doreen was tall and pale and thin with long, black hair cut in a Cleopatra fringe. We held hands in the playground and kept fear at arm's length as best we could by sharing talk and toys. Doreen was my first friend. We'd endure a lot together, especially throughout our final three school years.

In P1 we copied down the endless letters and numbers that marched across the blackboard. With thick, black pencils cocked in our clumsy fists, we patterned pages with 'walking-stick Fs' and 'fat-men 5s'. My jotter was a marvel of disorder, showing all those fitful attempts at accuracy. I would force the pencil so hard onto a page that its grooved impression could be seen on all those underneath. Then the shame of a silly mistake was rubbed with such frenzy that not only the flawed letter disappeared but the very paper itself, leaving damning evidence in the shape of a big, smudgy hole. Miss would give me an admonitory tap on the hand and sigh at my red face and threatened tears, and I'd guiltily turn to a clean page and start again.

Relief from such rigour came in the form of a great fulvous ball of Plasticene and a board. My classmates and I spent many happy afternoons rolling out long sausages and shaping them into people and dogs. What an industry this was: palms moving together in circular motions to make bodies and heads, our stubby fingers stumbling over the more delicate demands of noses, eyes and ears.

Before hometime Miss would read us a story as the fire died. She'd open a big, shiny book on her lap and tell us about fairies or goblins, or sometimes the man named Jesus. She was on her favourite territory then; I was to hear a whole lot more about Him in the near future.

Miss McKeague's choice of career had obviously been arrived at after much soul-searching. I believe she'd pondered deeply the confines of the convent before settling on the relative freedom of the classroom. I can picture her as a young girl: head bowed over steepled fingers, kneeling at the altar in pious supplication, asking the Good Lord for guidance. Her final choice seemed a fitting compromise, promising God that as a teacher she would do all in her power to instil His message in her pupils.

To say that she was a religious zealot would be an understatement because the nun within the educator was forever to the fore. Under her tutelage I learned more about Catholicism than I would at any other time in my life. Too much too soon is a recipe for disaster, so much so that these days I can only describe myself as 'a recovering Catholic'.

The RE lesson started at nine and ended at three, or so it seemed. There were morning prayers, mid-morning prayers, grace before meals, grace after meals, then the RE lesson proper, which lasted longer than any other, and finally prayers before hometime. We might have had difficulty with the two-times table or the spelling of our own name, but any such faltering with the Our Father or Hail Mary was the gravest sin of all, and a very good reason for our orisons to be repeated ad nauseam.

We were floored by Christ's Passion and invigorated by his Resurrection. There was an extravagance about Miss then which no other subject could evoke; the dramatic gesturing of crossing and breast-beating of herself as she told of His gruelling journey to Calvary and final expiation. She wept real tears then and we did too, as only children can, trying to understand His suffering and wondering all the while how we could have caused it. I would see His bloodstained face and beseeching eyes every day as He looked down on me from the glossy scroll that hung on the classroom wall, and was conscious always that Jesus was watching me closely for the merest sign of weakness.

Miss had the ability to fuel our fantasies to an intoxicating degree. Heaven was where it all happened. The boys could drive around for all eternity in pink Cadillacs and we girls could wear frothy white gowns with matching wings and golden crowns. At the wave of a silver wand, showers of sweets would pour from an ever-blue sky. There would be rivers of chocolate and mountains of cake and the sun would always shine. We all yearned to go there, but there was just one small problem: we had to die first. And not only that, we had to die in a 'state of grace'. So we learned our prayers fervently and struck our chests harder with our tiny fists, knowing that the more we prayed and suffered, the speedier would be our entry into paradise.

Not surprisingly, all this religious brainwashing took up so much room in my head that it tended to block out the rudiments of my early education. And no more so than when I reached P4 and was required to undergo the twin terror-inducing ordeals of confession — the fearful preamble to First Holy Communion — and the Religious Examination.

Our teacher was nothing if not inventive, improvising with a cup of water in place of wine, and pieces of ice-cream wafer for the host. We stood in a solemn circle, sipped the water, threw back our heads, stuck out our tongues and waited for the proffered wafer. Afterwards there was a tense silence as we hung our heads and contemplated the wafer doing its work of pouring all that grace and goodness into us.

I was looking forward to the pomp and ceremony of my First Communion. Nobody, however, had told me about the reality of confession. Confessing sins to Miss was easy, but nothing quite prepares a young child for the tyranny of the confessional — the inky darkness, the stranger behind the grille and the stilted litany of one's misdeeds.

Father Monacle's confession box had been designed for adults, not for very short people or little children like me. I entered its dark interior and, obeying Miss's instructions to the letter, knelt down on the prie-dieu — and disappeared from view. The bewildered priest waited and waited. I heard a tentative 'Yes, my child?' and became so petrified that I could not get up. Miss had impressed upon us that we must always remain kneeling in the sight of God and the priest.

On getting no response, the good Father stuck his head out the cubicle door.

'Who's next?' he asked gruffly.

A lady at the head of the waiting row blushed fiercely, got up at once and entered the confessional – to find me cowering there. She hesitated.

'What's this?' Father Monacle roared at me. 'What are you doin' down there, in the name of God?'

'M–Miss s–said—'

'What!'

'Miss said I was to kneel down, so she did, and I—'

'Miss isn't the priest, is she?'

'No, Father.'

'Well, tell Miss that I said it's all right if you stand up on the kneeling board from now on.'

'Yes, Father.'

'So I hope you're not going to waste any more of my precious time, are ye?'

And with that I was hotly dismissed with a very red face and a decade of the rosary to be said right up at the altar.

Every penitent in the waiting row knew that to be given the rosary and the altar by Father Monacle implied that you had done some serious sinning indeed.

It was a bad beginning and I was determined from that day on never to put a foot wrong when it came to our parish priest and his confessional. I continued to intone that oft-repeated preamble 'Bless me, Father, for I have sinned; this is *my first confession*' when I must surely have been on my twenty-first. It shows how well I'd ingested the mantra, how little I understood the whole sorry charade and, most importantly of all, how fearful I was of committing the sin of disobedience and actually thinking for myself.

My First Communion was a triumphant affair. I was all got up in a lacy white dress and veil, white patent-leather shoes and matching handbag, and carried the essential accessories of every aspiring young Catholic girl: a prayer-book with a pearlised cover and plastic rosary beads. The book, with its gilt edging and lettering proclaiming *My Holy Missal*, had been purchased by my thrifty mother in a 1960s' equivalent of today's Poundstretcher. It was printed — or rather misprinted — in Belgium, with amusing consequences. Here and there an 'a' would mysteriously be replaced by an 'o'. That missal would help me to relieve the boredom of many a Sunday mass — I would fervently entreat the Lord to 'wosh owoy' my sins.

In my white frock and matching accessories I looked like a miniature bride and felt like a fairytale princess. I believe there's a conspiracy afoot within the Church with regard to young girls. We're given the sensation of that white frock and veil so early in life. It acts as the proverbial dangling carrot and gives the dream of marriage focus.

Not that I entertained such thoughts that day. As I stood at the altar in my finery it seemed to me that all the difficult days of preparation had been worthwhile. Simply to wear the frock — and be made to feel special for once, no matter how fleetingly — was a reward in itself.

With Communion done and dusted, Miss McKeague focused all her energies on preparing us for the Religious Exam, a yearly test conducted by the fearsome Father Monacle. It seemed to have no other purpose than to ensure that we were in no danger of even *thinking* about consorting with the Evil One.

Certainly we children could have done without it, but for our teacher it was yet another excuse to neglect 'less important' subjects, such as history and geography. After all, what was more relevant to a Catholic child: knowing about the world or knowing who had made it?

Our green-covered, dog-eared catechisms of Christian doctrine were learned by heart and we fought feverishly to retain it all in our wee heads until the dreaded day arrived.

   Q. Who made the world?
   A. God made the world.
   Q. Who is God?
   A. God is our Father in Heaven, the Creator and Lord of all things.
   Q. How many persons are there in the one God?
   A. There are three persons in the one God: the Father, the Son and the
      Holy Ghost.

Miss rehearsed the questions, guiding us with a pencil waved dramatically in the air like a conductor's baton. We sang out our responses, sometimes falling out of tune — due to inattention or, more probably, temporary brain paralysis — but managing always to end together on an ear-popping crescendo. Most of what was taught and learned was delivered in this lilting manner so that eventually the words took on a meaningless life of their own.

> And for ever and ever Amen,
> And two times twelve makes twenty-four,
> And they all lived happily ever after.

Rote-learning had turned us all into performing parrots. The pedagogical aim of my early schooling seemed to be 'learn by heart first and understand later'. We were word-perfect though confused, but what did that matter?

Miss always appeared a wee bit flustered on the morning of the great event, the Exam. After all, her very probity was at stake; she could not be seen to falter in the eyes of the good priest, nor could any of us. When the sharp rap sounded on the door we all scrambled to attention. Silence fell like a great blanket as *he* entered.

I'd seen Father Monacle before in the dim light of the confessional, and from a distance as he celebrated Sunday mass (for most of the time with his back to us, in conformation with the Church wisdom of the time). Now I saw him at close quarters.

He was a heavily built man with an alarmingly bald head that shone, as if he'd used a buffing wheel on it that very morning. His eyes appeared huge and menacing behind bifocals, and his head and neck were all of a piece with a spreading purple hue. He looked like a great, black wine bottle, with his purple stopper head and white elliptical collar.

The air quivered with his stertorous breaths, the floorboards creaked under his substantial tread as he waded into the room. We watched and waited in the dreadful silence until he finally came to a halt at the front of the class.

Miss by this stage had begun to unravel, one hand fluttering to the back of her hair, the other smoothing down her skirt. She was swallowing hard, the brooch at her throat rising and falling with the rhythm of her anxiety. Father Monacle struck fear and holy terror into our wee hearts as he stood there, scanning our submissive little faces with his great searchlight eyes, probing for the slightest stain of sin. When at last he spoke it felt like a volcano erupting — a long, low rumbling that caused even our desks to tremble.

'Are they all good children, Miss McKeague?'

'Oh yes, Father!'

'What about young Lagan and McCloy down there? Learning, are they?'

'Yes, Father. Brendan and Michael are making good progress, Father.'

'Is that so, miss? Well, we'll see about that, won't we?'

And with that he was off on a tour of the room,

plucking out surnames and punching us with questions. Miss kept one pace behind him, her pained face and mouth working like a goldfish's, urging us on as we stammered and babbled our answers.

Everyone passed of course — that was part of the charade. Father Monacle would appear to soften as he prepared to leave. It seemed as if all the fear and panic he'd spread among us was gathered back into his great, black coat as he bestowed a beaming smile upon us and vented a hearty 'Well done, children!' Our little faces melted in the warmth of such praise and Miss gave a huge sigh of relief.

When he'd gone, Miss had an announcement to make.

'Because you've been such good children, I have a special reward for all of you.' And she ducked into her storeroom.

We waited in joyous anticipation, whispering among ourselves, each trying to outguess the other as to what this wonderful prize could be. Some thought money, others were convinced it would be sweets, and the general consensus favoured the latter.

Miss re-emerged moments later, clutching our trophies: a brand-new, plain brown pencil for each of us. It was a right miserable gift when you come to think of it. We'd set our hearts on a chocolate, or even an Imperial Mint from the frequently replenished little round tin on her desk, but it was not to be. We did get out to play, though, while Miss helped herself to a cup of very sweet tea and a Marie biscuit, no doubt to get her blood sugar levels back to normal, poor thing.

I fell into the school routine. Lunchtime was always a welcome incursion into the monotony of one's day, not least because a half-hour of freedom followed.

The playground was heaven for most of us. I learned to recognise those souls for whom it was purgatory, a thirty-minute respite from the headmaster, whose ire they'd called down upon themselves that day. They stood apart from us, cowed and with faces red from crying.

So far I had only experienced Master Bradley from the safety of Miss's room. Often we'd hear him shouting, then the sounds of the horrid slaps followed by the shrill screams of the victim. Miss would cross herself then and ask us to say a silent prayer. In the playground I saw the damage that had been done, and it was ugly.

My classmates and I lived in fear of crossing the tragic boundary between P4 and P5, between paradise and hell. All too soon I would know the ghastly truth, but for now we skipped, hopped and jumped with caution. Our hair slides and bows came undone, and our eyes and noses grew runny with exertion. We were permitted these lapses in decorum; all too soon we'd be returning to the discipline of the classroom. All too soon we'd hear Miss blow her whistle, followed by the hollow clapping of the Master's hands. Fun was over.

Looking back, I see that those first four years of childhood were easy. I none the less had no great urge to go to school. I hated having to leave my mother every morning to trudge with my brothers that four-mile journey, and was greatly curious as to what she did when the three of us were gone. I desperately wanted to return, believing that my absence left a void in her day. I know better now: she probably heaved a great sigh of relief at our retreating backs, turned to tend the baby and get on with her many tasks. Our departure meant remission of a sort for her.

On considering those early years, I see my mother forever occupied and busy and my father as an elusive figure who stood apart: stern, scornful and mostly silent.

There was little gaiety at home. During the day we played outside until the gathering darkness forced us indoors.

The only stimulus in our pre-television home was a green plastic record-player which the parents would take out on a Friday evening. On it my father would play the most insufferable renditions from the 'Republican hit parade' of the day, songs like *Sean South from Garryowen*. There was *Kevin Barry, Johnson's Motor Car* and — perhaps the most popular of all — *Up Went Nelson*, which celebrated the violent demolition of Nelson's Pillar in Dublin in March 1966. This burlesque opened with the deafening roar of a simulated explosion, a blast of sound which nearly blew the ears clean off us. We'd sit captive on the couch, listening to the thudding stridency of anthem after anthem, our impressionable minds being drip-fed Ireland's troubled history.

Christmas, though, made up for many ills. It was the festival that raised us into bliss, a time of light to brighten our lives as each gloomy year drew to a close.

Because mother had all the work to do in the run-up to the big day, she quite naturally began to communicate her frustration early on.

'There'll be no Christmas this year,' she'd say without fail. 'I'm not buying a damned thing. No turkey, no cake, no nothing. I'm sick of the whole damned lot of ye, so I am.'

Given what I now know about my overworked, cash-strapped mother, I can fully understand her frustration. To her, Christmas was more of a curse than a celebration. All the same my heart would lurch when I'd hear these protestations and I'd worry right up until the big day itself, in case she'd carry out her threat.

I need not have fretted. Christmas morning arrived like a dream fulfilling my every wish. Santa Claus always delivered. Mother would have drawn nine chalk circles on the floor, each with a name attached, and Santa would know which toys to pile in which circle. The empty milk jug and a few crumbs of mince-pie left on the table proved beyond doubt that he'd rested awhile in our humble kitchen before continuing his journey.

I was overjoyed with my doll and plastic jewellery, the jigsaw and the *Bunty Annual*. How many hours did I spend gazing at the cover, wondering if I could train our collie Carlo to jump through hoops just like Bunty's dog could? The impossible radiance of that one day of the year cannot be dimmed no matter how many decades pass. Strangely enough, I realised even then that it was my mother who had made it all happen. By late morning I was so full of chocolate I could not face dinner, and instead sat at the table watching Aunt Margaret try to eat hers.

Margaret was an attractive woman in her forties who stood in for the aunt we never had. She was a cousin of mother's and an essential feminine presence to offset the drabness of our many uncles. She was a stiff woman with legs as thin as dowelling rods. Feet in flat, suede slip-ons, never high heels: 'It's me bunions, Mary', wore dimpled gloves and a coat with a mandarin collar. Her hair was her best feature: thick and shiny, inexpertly tamed with castor oil and a brush. She had chosen not to marry, and this was looked upon as a character flaw rather than a conscious decision. My mother would say that Maggie 'had missed her markets' and vent a sigh of disapproval.

On Christmas Day she'd arrive clutching gifts that never varied from one year to the next: a jam sponge in a cardboard box from Ditty's Bakery in Maghera and a bottle of Harvey's Bristol Cream sherry. There was always a vague air of helplessness about her, as though she were forever searching for something she knew she'd never find. This persistent questing was also brought to the dinner table; she couldn't sit on a hard chair, always needed a cushion: 'It's me piles, Mary.' Every Christmas a different part of Margaret ached. We heard about bunions, corns, ulcers, wind and cramp. She ate very little, perhaps for all these reasons, and would poke and search among the contents of the plate to see if that elusive something might be trapped under a slice of turkey or among the vegetables.

After dinner she and my parents chatted by the fire, becoming more animated with the sherry, while we played with our toys — breaking most of them. It was plain, even to us children, that Aunt Margaret had never perfected the art of conversation. My mother would make a simple enquiry and could have gone off and said a couple of rosaries before Margaret got round to answering. After what seemed like an interminable silence, she'd say something like 'What was that, Mary?' before reverting to her usual, detached self. Her solitary life had left her unable to communicate.

Television changed all that, and Christmas afternoons became less of a trial for everyone concerned. Not that I had much say in my viewing matter; the adults would decide what was suitable entertainment. Five of us would squeeze onto the couch with Margaret teetering at one end, and watch the most mind-numbing selection of programmes imaginable: *The Black and White Minstrel Show* (our visitor's favourite), *Seven Brides for Seven Brothers* (mother's favourite) and *They Flew to Bruges* (father's).

After hours of tedious television, sweet cake, idle talk and syrupy sherry Margaret would have metamorphosed from timid and uneasy to red-cheeked and tipsy, and would be 'helped' out to the car to be driven back to her council semi in Maghera.

However, no matter how boring the television became there was always the distraction of a jigsaw or the prospect of yet more sweets. Christmas Day never failed to make me happy. It was the one day that guaranteed complete and utter joy.

The 25 December 1966 was no exception. It hardly prepared me for the year to follow, though. That September I was entrusted to the not-so-tender care of Master Bradley.

Lessons in Hell

If Miss was the rewarding angel then Master Bradley was surely the avenging one. No two personalities could have been more divergent. I was passed from the ease of the one into the fearful clutches of the other. This was when the unravelling of my innocence began. In the Master's room I learned so much about fear and terror that no space was left for anything else.

Master Bradley was a tall, thin man, bald with a lick of crowning hair that stood up in the wind as he marched around the playground. His gaunt face, pale eyes and mean, striated mouth rarely softened into a smile, but frequently quivered into a rictus of joy when he beat us. He smoked lavishly and often; his sickly pallor and ochreous fingers bore the evidence. From the safety of my desk I'd watch him light up an endless succession of Gallaher Greens, steadying the flaming match in a cupped claw and sucking greedily — giving life to the fag while shortening his own.

Every child who sat before him was in the line of fire — we were the collateral damage of his insidious temper and frustration. It didn't take much to set him off. We could be beaten for the most harmless errors: scraping back our chairs accidentally, forgetting to address him as 'sir', not coming up quick enough to his desk when summoned. The list was as varied as his moods, and the more erratic the mood the more vicious would be the blows he'd rain down on innocent heads and hands and legs.

I got beaten for not answering loudly enough, for bungling a line of my nine-times table; for stumbling over the eleventh stanza of *The Rime of the Ancient Mariner* — yes the *eleventh* — for missing one spelling in a list of 20; for neglecting to stand up when spoken to; for dropping my books, for crying, for talking, for fidgeting. In other words: I was punished for being my cowardly, helpless, fear-driven self. In hindsight I understand the tactics of the bully. He'll flog what he despises most in others, to stymie those same qualities in himself. But the fury is rarely quenched; the fire rages on.

Sometimes he'd be late, and Miss — never one to neglect an opportunity for piety — would step over the threshold and lead the juniors and us in morning prayers. Oh, how I wished I could have gone back with her! And how well I remember the egg-beater churnings in my stomach as I prayed earnestly and fervently that Master Bradley would not show. Occasionally my prayers would be answered, but those days were rare indeed. No, like as not we'd hear the engine die, the car door slam and his head would appear at the farthest window, the wisp of hair waving in nasty reproach as he marched down the slope, his profile sinking lower at each successive window as if the very ground were swallowing him up. How we wished it would!

He'd stride into the room, bringing all his rancour with him: our judge, jury and 'executioner'.

> Well had the boding tremblers learn'd to trace
> The day's disasters in his morning face.

The register was taken first. He would open a tall, red bound ledger and, with a splayed hand and cocked pen, run down the list, flinging out our surnames. If you didn't respond loudly enough he repeated your name in an amplified roar, glaring up maniacally from the page. The bullets of invective would fly.

'Get out of the wrong side of the bed, McKenna?' he asked me one cold, November morning.

'No, sir.'

'Asleep, are you?'

'No, sir.'

'What was that?' And he cocked a hand to his ear and strained his head to one side in mock deference.

'No, sir – sorry, sir.'

'I didn't hear that.'

'No, sir.' I tried to respond more loudly, my voice rising to a faltering whine.

'No sir *what*?' he roared.

'No, sir … I'm not asleep … I … I … didn't get out … of … of the side of the b–b–b–b–bed … this morning … (I heard the ripple of low laughter now from my nervous audience) … I … I … I mean the wrong side … '

I trailed off, mumbling and stumbling over words as the room began to blur.

'Stop bumbling, McKenna.'

Then came the words I didn't want to hear.

'Come up here … Now!'

And my fate was sealed yet again.

I'd cry as I made that harrowing journey, the shuddering sobs making my shoulders rise and fall in jerks of great despair as I trudged to his desk. And all the while his predatory gaze followed me until that moment of dread when I offered up my trembling palms. He took tremendous care in the positioning of them, manoeuvring them to the desired height with the aid of the stick, eyeing the level, angling his feet like a prizefighter for a more dynamic blow. And all the while I wept, and all the while he ignored my tears.

The first stinging wallops would cause my hands to drop. He'd prod them back into position, and whack again — and perhaps again, depending on how enraged he felt. There was a deathly silence in the room then because everyone felt my terror and wondered fearfully who'd be next.

The punishment finished, Master Bradley would glare at me as I made my slow retreat to the desk. Only when I'd taken my seat would he return, calmly, to the register and continue the roll-call.

I'd sit there resting the swollen hands on my lap, the spasms of pain riffling through me from head to toe, my cheeks searing under the tightening wash of tears. And he would not allow me my essential grief.

'McKenna, if you don't stop blubbering you'll get the same again.'

I'd stop immediately, and for the rest of the day shut down all the accesses to my sorrow, my head pounding with the injustice, the words I wanted to scream and shout stuck in my throat, choking me into silence. At playtime I'd become one of those lost souls I'd seen when in Miss McKeague's care, the ones in purgatory. I'd stand alone by the school wall and no one would venture to play with me, so fearful were they of inviting the same wrath upon themselves by the sin of association.

'McKenna' was all I ever got from him; none of us was ever given the dignity of being addressed by our first name. This was another cruel ploy to further reduce our fragile self-esteem. Some of the boys — whom he loathed more than the girls — didn't even merit that, but were given biblical nicknames: Isaac, Job, Jacob *et al.* The Master seemed to find this terribly amusing.

He was like my father: sombre, remote, disingenuous, with a cruel streak. They both liked to see others suffer.

I had the same sense of dread and foreboding at home as I did in school. But at home I had mother to run to. In school I had no one.

The Master's hawthorn stick was symbolic of his twisted discontent. Faithfully, each September, he'd select one specially from the hedge that braided the playing field. We'd observe him as we played; he'd study the shrubbery with forensic interest, like a botanist hunting a rare species. For not any old stick would do; it had to be straight, and studded with a healthy rash of thorns, all the better for a more tactile response. Having spotted a suitable specimen, he'd cut it free with his penknife and carry it indoors under his arm. We'd stop our play and watch him go, following him with anxious eyes and accelerating heartbeats.

During that first week of the new school year, while we covered our books and wrote our names big on the covers, the Master would devote every spare moment to honing and paring the new instrument of cruelty, sharpening the punishing points and reddening them with a marker. In my blameless head I saw it twisted and turned into that crown of blood and thorns, and realised I would have to suffer just like Him.

For school was largely suffering, and little else. I did not learn much from my oppressor; few of us did. His perversion had succeeded in stalling the learning process. My pencils and rulers became for me instruments of torture; and my books, with their lines of spellings and verses and stories, manuals of sheer frustration. Fear and its brother Shame had taken hold of my heart to an awesome degree. All their insidious by-products — anxiety, shyness, confusion and woe — began to coalesce in me like so many heavy stones; they were dragging me down, to keep me alone, resistant and unreachable for a long time to come.

My classmates and my siblings all endured the same degree of unwarranted and inexcusable pain. When we weren't receiving it from Master Bradley we were witnessing the violence done to others. That unholy trinity of receiving, witnessing and the consequent suffering was always to the fore.

The only defence my fear-stricken mind could offer was the comfort and protection of the prayers Miss had taught me. Each morning on our four-mile hike to school, whether in hail, rain or sun, I prayed that I wouldn't upset the Master; prayed that he wouldn't ask me a question; prayed that I wouldn't give a wrong answer; prayed that I wouldn't have to ask to go to the toilet, prayed that I could hold all my fear and water in until breaktime or playtime or hometime, because the Master did not like to be disturbed.

My head throbbed from running this bitter narrative. I had headaches on the way to school and again on the way back, what with the thought of homework I couldn't do, the thought that mother would shout and father would be in bad form (she frequently did, and he frequently was) and — perhaps the most hurtful thought of all — the certainty that there was no one to help or console me. My brothers and sisters could not assist me. They were feeling the scourge of the injustice as keenly as I was.

Deliverance from the tyrannical Master would arrive on occasion when Miss Heron, a replacement teacher, was slotted in if Bradley was ever off sick. Mother used to say he was 'bad with the nerves' — which was not surprising.

The Misses Heron and McKeague were similar in appearance: they were spinsters and both favoured the dove-grey and slate-blue suits that matched their hair. There, sadly, the similarities ended. Miss McKeague was all leanness, dedication and piety; Miss Heron was large, indolent and for the most part indifferent.

She was a courageous dresser, had a penchant for the knitted two-piece, a necessity for the fuller figure in those pre-Lycra days; it was the only fabric that could adequately stretch its way round her generous bosom and hips. She accessorised the suits with strings of pearls, a capacious banana-coloured handbag, and a pair of sandals in the same shade.

On learning that Miss Heron had been 'teaching' us my mother would comment that the lady in question was 'terrible good with her hands', no doubt alluding to her skill with the knitting needles.

Yet it was clear to me, even back then, that Miss Heron had a rather limited grasp of teaching methodology. She would sit at the Master's table, reading either *Ireland's Own* or *The People's Friend* while we got on with our work. She never engaged in active teaching, and that was her loss as well as ours. Her only reason for leaving the desk was to forage surreptitiously in the store cupboard where she'd stow a supply of chocolate biscuits. These demands for sustenance were prompted by boredom rather than hunger. Her handbag, too, contained a hoard of Merimaids which she popped covertly when she thought no one was looking. We always knew of course; the crackling wrappers betrayed her.

Her approach to instruction was a simple, all encompassing one: getting us to do as much work as possible without expending any energy herself. She'd write the following in a generous hand on the board, and ask us not to disturb her until we were finished.

Copy pages 33–40 from Bible [RE]
Draw map of Ireland and label [geography]
Draw a picture of the Blessed Virgin Mary and colour in [art]
Write a story about your picture of the BVM [English]

She didn't seem to be too keen on maths, and that was fine by me because I was a right dunce when it came to sums.

Miss Heron also had quite an imaginative interpretation of extracurricular activities. One such involved a pair of Bakelite binoculars and a box of sepia-tinted slides. We were summoned to a table at the front in family groups; those with several brothers and sisters in the room went first. My two brothers and I were usually second.

The slides we viewed consisted mainly of ladies in big hats, soldiers and airmen with beaver moustaches, and Lancaster bombers taking off and landing. Miss Heron never actually explained what we were looking at, and we didn't ask, so pleased were we to be out of our seats, and relieved that we weren't likely to get the heads and hands 'bate off us'.

But we were always sad when she departed, because her going could only mean the demon's return. We didn't learn much from her but felt completely safe in her presence as she sat there like a big, dumpy frog, chewing her sweets and scanning the mags. We could take liberties then, passing each other cinnamon lozenges and clove rock – the latter being the M&M's of the sixties – and swapping copies of *Judy* or *The Beano*, knowing that she barely had the inclination to rise, let alone the energy to give us a clout.

Master Bradley was a blight on our entire school year, and few were the people and occasions that granted us a reprieve. One very welcome diversion stands out in my memory: Varnie the Magic Man.

Each year, with a show that lasted a good and unforgettable hour, Varnie would turn up to entertain us. Great was our joy when the Master announced that everyone was to bring in one and sixpence on the following Friday, to cover Varnie's costs.

The thought of the Magic Man's arrival made us so excited that we could fleetingly forgive Master Bradley his outbursts — and that speaks volumes about Varnie. His hour gave us such happiness that he restored our faith in the adult of the species and lifted us up, however temporarily, into that enchanted realm where we believed everything was possible.

Nothing could compare with the excitement that accompanied the Magic Man's arrival. We'd hear the thunder of Varnie's motorbike and our ears would prick up. The Master would then instruct us to put away our books and sit up straight. Two boys — how the rest of the class envied them! — were dispatched to help Varnie carry in the black boxes which contained the tools of his trade.

He always dressed for the occasion in an obligatory and suitably mysterious black suit. It had obviously never seen the inside of a dry-cleaner's in its long history, the alarming shine on knees and elbows almost complementing the satin braiding of trouser-legs and lapels. Under this he wore a shocking-pink shirt with a ruched and frilly front. When his performance grew heated he'd discard the jacket with a great flourish, to reveal the shirt in its full glory.

He was a little fat man, in profile reminiscent of a plump blackbird. His hair was sparse; he wore it greased and stretched over a yeasty forehead. I suspect that Brylcreem always topped Varnie's toiletry list. With his fleshy face and oily moustache and hair, he looked like a latter-day Hercule Poirot.

In retrospect his repertoire, though truly magical to us then, was spectacularly mundane; it involved for the most part a walking stick, a top hat and a rubber chicken. There was also a great deal of scarf-waving, card-shuffling and coin-flipping.

The finale was memorable because of its daftness. Varnie would select six boys and give each one a tubular bell and a little bar with which to strike it. The bells were of differing lengths, each having its own note, and the idea was that Varnie could invoke a tune from the boys simply by tapping each one on the shoulder at certain intervals. That, at least, was the theory — but it rarely worked in practice, whether on account of one boy's inability to strike his instrument on cue or lack of alertness on the part of the others. After several attempts Varnie would become very frustrated indeed, his face turning as shockingly pink as his shirt, and in the end he'd simply give up. It was all one to us, of course; we didn't care how it sounded as long as we were being entertained.

Throughout all this frivolity the Master would sit in the corner, smoking one furious cigarette after another and reading a copy of the *Irish News*. He would, at last, rouse himself after the finale — when Varnie had decided he'd had enough and was taking a low bow with a sweeping flourish. We'd cheer and applaud for as long as we could, making the moment last, until the roar of the Master put paid to our enthusiasm. Then it was time for us to offer up our hot coinage from hands that had gone sweaty with excitement. That excitement and appreciation was truly from the heart.

On our way home from school that day we'd come across Varnie, reclining on a grass verge by the side of the road with his mighty bike parked behind him. There he'd be: counting his takings and chuckling happily to himself. We somehow knew that we were witnessing a very private moment and would softly tiptoe past.

Varnie made me forget my fear. For that hour I got lost in the bewitching world of make-believe. For most of those days in school I was the passive absorber of dreary facts. Learning was a chore because it was presented as a burden to be shouldered rather than an adventure to be enjoyed. I could not become engrossed in Master Bradley's classes. The fear of being beaten for no reason overshadowed any sense of healthy curiosity about the world. I loved to draw and I loved to sing, but the Master was very rarely in the mood to allow us to indulge in such diversions. Had Bradley had his way completely then even those rare visits from people like Mr O'Leary, the dancing teacher, would never have taken place.

Mr O'Leary appeared at the school when I'd reached P7, the final year. No doubt the education authorities had dispatched him to nurture latent artistic talent. I got the chance to shine, if only temporarily.

Mr O'Leary came to teach us Irish dancing. He was nowhere near as exciting as Varnie, of course, but was a welcome distraction just the same. Every Thursday at precisely 12.15 he would arrive in a ready-made suit, carrying a vinyl-plastic tape recorder. He held himself as erect as an army major, face like a stone, hair oiled flat. He was restless. He was keen; didn't walk but skipped. Those feet were made for dancing, heels for clicking, toes for pointing, his life one endless hornpipe.

Without warning he'd launch into a demonstration reel or jig. It looked as though an electric shock had passed right through him. He'd go completely rigid from the waist up, stare straight ahead of him, and kick his legs high, while doing a circuit of the room.

He'd then call on us to imitate him. We did so in pairs, and I think we managed it without much difficulty. Only when he turned on the music, however, did we lose all coordination and memory of the steps. Pandemonium broke loose. The boys blundered about with the grace of hippos: kicking, stepping on toes, and colliding with one another. We girls spent our time sidestepping an array of their size-ten plastic sandals and smelly slippers.

This horseplay did not amuse Mr O'Leary. He'd turn off the music with an angry snap and set about winnowing the graceful from the graceless, sending the offenders back to their seats.

And joy! He decreed that I — yes, little me — had an ear and a feel for dance. He would often use me to demonstrate how things should be done. At last I had found something I could excel in. But sadly nothing ever came of this latent talent; my mother didn't seem to think that proficiency in Irish dancing was such an impressive asset, so the potential in my little legs was never realised. It might have meant an important confidence booster but it was not to be. Culture of any description did not figure large in Lisnamuck.

Those rare and delightful intrusions — Miss Heron's slide show, Varnie's magic, Mr O'Leary's dancing — exemplified a world I seldom glimpsed. They each afforded me flashes of experience I should have had in greater measure: joy, merriment, freedom and lightness. Are they not the very things a child needs in order to grow in spirit?

There seemed to be so much anger in the air in my childhood. I felt the same degree of hostility both at home and at school. The only conclusion I could draw at that early age was that I was causing it. I internalised this and grew to believe that I was wicked and unworthy, and therefore helpless in the face of it; I was left not knowing how to make things right and all those angry adults happy.

School was not all doom and gloom; there was at least one hour of the week when I was happy, 60 precious minutes when Master Bradley did not hold sway. For the last hour on a Friday afternoon we got to do needlework with Miss McKeague.

Nothing could compare with the relief I felt at being excused from the Master's presence with the words, 'Would the girls now slip quietly into their sewing.' The word 'quietly' was superfluous here: each of us was a model of subordination. Yet the Master always felt the need to remind us just the same.

In Miss's sewing class I was forever knitting a red scarf. This joyous labour seemed to stretch over four years, with a multitude of dropped stitches and tangled knots along the way.

We would sit in a semicircle round the stove, our shins mottling in the heat, our pink faces lowered and tongue-tips appearing through lips tightened with effort. And, as the crackling fire and clacking needles carried on a noisy dispute with each other, it didn't matter if the sun shone or the rain fell; for that hour of the fearsome school week I was happy.

I was happy because I was in safe territory, away from the ill-tempered jolts and stabbing gaze of the Master. In Miss's room I could drop a stitch without the risk of being beaten. Her customary reaction was to gently free the wool from my hands and repair the damage as best she could.

With Miss I knew I could make mistakes and be forgiven, that I could ask permission to go to the toilet and not be refused. My limbs felt looser, my head lighter, and my words flowed more freely.

As I sat there I sometimes thought about the boys and girls who had, like me, sat at that stove — or one very much like it — trying to make sense of that little part of Ulster we inhabited. This was the school my parents and relatives had endured all those years before. Had their teachers been any different? Perhaps. I wondered if they, as children, had sat there like me, tightened in by unknowing, with all their dreams before them 'spread out like a spring-woken tree'.

Unhappy Home

Our house stood in the shadow of the Glenshane mountain range, three miles east of predominantly Catholic Draperstown, two miles north of Protestant Tobermore, and five or so miles from Maghera, which nurtured a risky mix of both. Such clearly delineated boundaries along lines of religion seemed just as important back then as they are now. The people of the locality liked to know where they — and their neighbours — stood.

This South Derry region is mainly farming country, studded with freeholds that have witnessed generation-long internecine conflict. Land and religion are of equal importance to the Ulster Catholics. This obsession with the soil is rooted in the dark past, when their forebears, being dispossessed during the Plantations, had to buy back their plots from the Protestant British. The sons of farming fathers therefore live together in an uneasy alliance, waiting for the 'holy ground' to one day pass to them. Where there is land there is discord; nowhere was this more in evidence than in my father's bleak ancestry.

On a piece of land ceded to him by his family he built the bungalow that would house us all, and reluctantly farmed the land that would feed and sustain us into adulthood. I say reluctantly because from the earliest age I was aware that my father did not want me. He'd wanted none of us; we were the unfortunate by-products of the marriage bed, the burdensome extras that forced him into a life of labour, rather than one of indolence, more fitting to his natural mien.

My parents, as seen in their wedding picture, bore little resemblance to the two people I came to know. My father was tall, rawboned and dour. His thick, black hair was combed severely back and fixed in place by a felt hat, shed only on Sundays and when eating. The eyes were blue and staring; one would need a raft of cold adjectives to describe their colour and intensity. The meagre mouth and narrow face rarely surrendered a smile.

As a child I do not remember a single encouraging word from him, a comforting arm around me if I fell and hurt myself, a smile of approval, an unexpected gift, a birthday card, a hug. He remained morose, pessimistic and a stranger to me always.

There were six boys in father's family; he was the third-born. From all accounts they were the progeny of a loveless union and a harsh childhood. They grew up in the cold, post-war atmosphere of the 1920s; from the earliest age they were treated not as children but used as little slaves to do the heavy housework and farm labouring.

They had proceeded from sunless children to barren bachelors: a yawning sombre procession trudging along one of life's more aimless paths, each one reticent and uneasy until my poor mother happened along. She naively chose my father and stumbled blindly and all too willingly into wedlock.

His brothers never forgave father for this transgression, an enmity they extended to us children as well. A suspicious eye and a grim look were all we received from our uncles; there were no pennies of reward, no smiles of approval, no words of comfort, not ever; just the accusatory, glaucous stare, especially from Uncle Robert, the Master. He was the bursar, the man who held the purse-strings.

You would think that marriage and children would have softened my father, but that wasn't the case. The accumulation and hoarding of the money, and getting his hands on the acreage, were as important to him as ever. But he now realised that since committing the sin of marriage he was even less favourably disposed. His wife and children were to blame for thwarting his access to the family fortune. We became a needless expense, and for this he actively resented us.

My poor mother attempted to compensate for his deficiencies, but hers was a relentless battle. Her photogenic beauty had saddened and drooped under the weight of his injustice, but she carried on being mother and father to all of us while he watched the show from the sidelines.

She was the physical force that woke us, washed us, clothed and fed us, before putting us on the road to school, while he slumbered selfishly on. She was the cook — pounding, churning, peeling, baking — and the one who trained us to eat properly at table. She was the cleaner: sweeping, mopping, and scrubbing our soiled nappies and clothes in basins of soapy water. She was the seamstress who knitted sweaters, darned socks, and stitched our floral frocks on her second-hand Singer sewing machine. She was the nurse who bandaged our cut knees, wiped our tears, and put us to bed with an aspirin crushed between two spoons and mixed in with jam.

And as if that wasn't enough, she was the chaperone who took us in to see doctors, opticians and dentists, while our father remained outside in the car. She was the gardener who planted and plucked and weeded to make the place look presentable.

She was the down-trodden wife who would carry tea to him only to hear him declare that it wasn't sweet enough, and he'd send her back for more sugar. She was the typical Irish mother of her time, dominated by the overbearing, crude actions of a thoughtless husband and cowed by the misogyny of the Church.

This litany of labour was the indispensable, inexhaustible language of her life; it fuelled, understandably, a rush of anger and dissatisfaction that she gave voice to at every turn. She shouted and cried with all the bitter force of a wind across the tundra, never silent, never static — she externalised everything.

It seemed that when she was on the move she was alive, goaded by his inertness. His torpor was her vigour, raging down the years.

There was a stubborn conspiracy between them, the indolent imploding of one exploding into the frenzied action of the other. He could sit for hours on the sofa eyeing a ruminative cow in a distant field while she fizzed and surged around him. He could just about find the energy to raise his feet off the floor as she swept and mopped under him. He knew this annoyed her and would say, in his defence: 'There's no need for half of that cleanin' atall, atall.' And we'd wait for the skirl of abuse.

My mother had three key utterances that she squawked out with such frequency that they resound in the memory still. One: 'I rue the day I married that man.' And she meant it, she truly did, every sinewy, rank syllable of it. Two: 'My heart's a breakin'.' I didn't doubt it. Since our father didn't love us we made up for the deficit by forever feasting on her heart. And finally the cry that stung the most: 'I may give this place up.' By this she meant the prison that was home and its sorry contents — all of us.

They were the sentiments of a wounded woman, defeated by the demands of being a wife and mother in

1960s' Ireland, who'd wed in the hope of finding contentment and joyous escape, only to discover a wilderness of despair. Now instead of just being the put-upon skivvy to a flock of brothers, she had a flock of children and a shiftless husband to boot. Because of this inequity she bickered fluently and repeatedly with the source of her pain: her husband, my father, and our lives became subordinate to her searing frustration and his cold dispassion.

The house I was born in was the standard bungalow of its time: three bedrooms, a kitchen, a scullery and a bathroom.

The three bedrooms were divided by hierarchy and gender: my parents in the biggest one, five girls and four boys sharing the smaller ones. Space was tight and tempers hot as we fought for our share of that space. Being the youngest girl I usually ended up as sandwich-filling between two sisters, lying straight as a rod with the bedclothes stretched across me; or I sometimes shared a narrow bed with another, wrestling for possession of a thin blanket, even to the point of holding its corner between gritted teeth to retain my territorial claim. As children we clashed for space and comfort and love, because all three were in short supply. When I left home I found that living alone was bliss.

It seemed that my mother never rested. The kitchen naturally was the focus of most of her activity. It was basic and functional (my father did not allow money to be spent on unnecessary things like cushions or frills). There was a scrubbed wooden table and eleven chairs, a brown vinyl couch, heavily studded along base and top with a seam of brass tacks, and cracked deeply into submission at one end, due to my father's frequent rest periods. A hulking range jutted out onto the polished floor, making as much noise as my frazzled mother, spitting and hissing with the wood and coal it was fed each day.

That range was rarely idle. A kettle or saucepan was forever on the boil. Endless 'drops' of tea were made and potatoes were a staple at lunchtime. Every day during holidays and at weekends I watched a great pot of Golden Wonders or Kerr's Pinks splutter and fume at noon, the lid bubbling up with furious thrusts and sighing back down again, creating rivulets of steam that burst and sizzled their way across the angry hot plate.

A good portion of my mother's day was spent baking and cooking. On the floured surface of the scrubbed table she kneaded and rolled the dough for the daily batches of scones, carrying the floppy triangles to the fired griddle and patting down with her caked 'masonry' hands. This job could not be rushed or left, so she'd stand there, palette-knife at the ready, waiting, flipping over, and waiting again, before carrying the swollen farls to the cooling rack. Back and forth, back and forth she'd go, between table and stove, wearing a path, felling the hours, nursing her angst and woe. I wonder now how many miles she travelled between that table and stove in the course of her lifetime, just to give us our daily bread. When finished, she'd take down the goose wing that hung by the mantelshelf, and dust off the excess flour. The griddle was cooled on the floor before being returned to its nail behind the scullery door.

In the oven of that vast range she roasted red meats and chicken for the Sunday lunch. She also cooked what she commonly referred to as her 'oven-scone'. This was a mighty currant mountain which raised itself to hot perfection in the tarnished whiskey tray she used as a tin.

For special occasions such as Christmas and birthdays she baked buns and cakes, and I'd help. Like old-time cook's assistant Johnny Craddock I always got to do the menial tasks: measuring the flour, breaking the eggs into a bowl and greasing the tin. She would stand there mixing the ingredients with deceptive ease while I knelt on a stool beside her, the better to follow it all. It was all magical to me then: the process of turning the gloopy mixture into a delicious cake amazed me. I thought that mother was a wonder-worker, and in her way I suppose she was.

The scullery was the source of all this industry and the place I loved to explore. It housed a collection of pots, pans and large bowls, and the hundredweight bag of Early Riser flour which went to bake all those wondrous cakes and scones. It sat on a stool behind the scullery door, its furled top steadily drooping down the more mother baked.

She didn't like having us under her feet when she was working in the scullery and she'd send us out to play. Our yard was an area flanked by great whitewashed barns, and it signified freedom and escape from our incommodious dwelling. During summer holidays we'd let our playful imaginations run loose there, or in the triangular garden to the front of the house, and the fields beyond. We'd tumble out of the back door with the aromas of eggs and baking bread in our nostrils — only to be pulled up short by the stench of manure spread on a nearby field. But there were other smells to compensate: sometimes we'd catch the exhilarating fragrance of freshly mown grass.

That yard was my world. I knew by heart the topography of its landscape: the rise of chopped firewood at its farthest point, which held out the promise of warmth against colder days to come. A row of cowpats from barn door to field where the lazy bluebottles droned in a gauze of summer heat, lighting and straying in a ceaseless dance. I'd hold my nose and watch them, wondering how they could feed on the rotten cakes; all that lifting off and landing seemed to indicate a kind of circumscribed freedom I couldn't understand.

The grey Fergie tractor with its striated metal bonnet, like the breastplate of some superior Indian chief, stood to one side of the firewood. A circular saw did double duty: it split wood and its bench served as shelter for Carlo our collie. He could just about raise his head and gaze with bored weariness when we invaded the yard, then lay his chin back down again and continue his doze in the sawdust. This was the domain of the farmyard animal and we were the intruders, frequently scattering the hens with our exuberant horseplay. They let us know we weren't welcome, giving us fierce, sudden looks as they high-stepped away.

When I recollect those distant days it's the silence that I remember most: the potent absence of noise out of doors; utter quiet, save for the mooing of a hungry cow or the stammering notes of a bird.

We broke that silence with our shouts and songs. We busied ourselves with the activity of play, climbing trees to pluck plums and pears, playing games of hide-and-seek in the cool, cavernous barns and having tea parties on tea-chests covered with flour bags.

Sometimes we'd be sent to a nearby spring to fill a pail of drinking water. This was arduous work for small people, for O'Neill's well lay at the far end of a distant field. The journey there was easy enough, but coming back was fraught with difficulty. When we got to the well we'd spend ages on our hunkers, gazing down into that circle of shimmering sky reflected in the water. I was annoyed by the midges that skimmed and pocked its surface, aware also that this was heaven's reflection and that I might be as close to it as mere mortals could get.

Then suddenly the midges would rise and heaven break as we plunged the bucket in. The hard part was drawing it up again: we would struggle with the weight of its gurgling rebellion, and heft it onto the grassy rim.

We'd break our return trip with many stops, all out of breath. The handle of the bucket was knitting-needle thin and would dig into our soft hands. We'd alter our grip, thereby slopping the water into our wellies. Usually we'd arrive home with a much-depleted bucket; mother would give us a good telling off and send us right back to do it all over again.

Through the shifting days of summer we roamed the fields and lanes around the house, busying ourselves out of doors so that our mother could find peace within. We lassoed jam jars with baler twine and set off to the nearby Moyola river.

Unwary sticklebacks trapped themselves in our glass prisons, wriggling and struggling for the freedom they would never know again. Sometimes we were very lucky and would capture two in one jar. Cupping hands carefully around our trophies, we'd carry them proudly home to show mother. She wouldn't allow them in the house, though, so we'd line the jars up on an outside windowsill, studying their captive occupants until we tired of them. But more often than not the poor fish tired first and would already have turned belly up in defeat before darkness closed in.

I delighted in the river. That active, surging mass of water moved me more than the fixed hedges and meadows that hemmed it. I loved to sit on the rocks that jutted from the bank and plunge my legs in up to the knee, marvelling at the refracting pull of the water's gravity. The sun would glitter madly, stunning my eyes, and my ears took the swell and sway of the water's release. I was alive to nature then, alert to the tender violation of all of my senses.

The river was a metaphor for fearlessness and risk-taking as it plunged along its path to freedom; being near it made me believe I could touch those same qualities in myself. My mother always warned me not to go in but, away from her watchful eyes, I invariably did. However fleetingly, I wanted to be part of that clamour that had the power to cleanse and quench and sometimes take life.

These were the idle wanderings of my childhood; with no television or books to distract me, my love affair with nature was guaranteed.

We trudged to and from school with the seasons; in winter capped, gloved and belted against the cruel sleet and bitter gusts, our shoulders hunched against the onslaughts, eyes and noses weeping. On rare occasions, prodded into action by my mother, father would come to collect us in the wobbling Ford Popular. He wouldn't drive all the way to the school gate, however, but stop a good mile down the road, making us stumble in sodden file the rest of the way. We were 'bother' to him and this was his way of letting us know it.

Once in the car, we'd rattle home in silence. There were no enquiries from him as to how school had been or what we'd learned, just a morose and bad-tempered muteness that hung in the air like a poised axe. I'd sit in the back seat between my two brothers with the rising smell of damp wool and the sting of his cigarette smoke in my eyes. I wanted to talk but knew I dare not. As a rule you did not speak unless you were spoken to and father never initiated friendly conversation with us, only accusation and rebuke. So we'd listen to the drubbing of the rain on the car roof and the lazy swish of the wipers, gaze through the runnels of water and stippled panes that made a Seurat canvas of fields and trees, as the car shuddered its way home.

On our arrival mother would divest us of the soaking overcoats, arranging them on a clothes-horse by the range, where they steamed themselves dry.

Oh, how I hated those short, damp days of winter! In the evenings our kitchen took on a look of sublime squalor, like some Turkish den in the peasant quarter of Istanbul.

We all congregated there in the cloying warmth, the air heavy with the smell of boiling potatoes and stewed tea. Frequently the cramped space was encroached upon by lines of washing. Four drying rails suspended above the range would be draped with everything from bloomers to towels. These stalactites of fabric hung dangerously close to the range and trembled in clouds of water vapour from the bubbling pot. All this moisture made the polished floor a hazard to walk on and the windowpanes clammy. When supper was ended and homework done, boredom would drive me to those panes and I'd finger-paint graffiti into the condensation. I hungered for something nameless — peace, probably, or freedom — and in my frustration would turn away from the noise of the family huddle, press my face against the glass, look out into the darkness, and listen to the wind singing round the corners of the house.

I don't know which was worse: being forced out of bed in the early morning, to trek though the elements to journey's end where you knew the Master waited, flexing his cane — or coming home to the wordless father and fretting mother in the gathering darkness of that house.

The ritual of those evenings was supper, homework, rosary and bed. We did our homework by the faint glow of a 40-watt bulb high up in the ceiling, young eyes squinting in the gloom. Homework not completed at the table was finished under the bedclothes by the light of a torch.

Schoolwork was a real burden to me, especially sums. I worried about not being able to do them and, if I managed to complete them, worried whether I'd got them right. All night long they roamed in my head, robbing me of the peace a child's mind deserves. The spectre of the tyrant Master would rear up in my dreams.

The rosary followed homework as surely as night follows day: all knees down on the cold, tiled floor, with sets of beads fumbled out of pockets and purses. My mother was the initiator. She took an aggressive interest in our religious affairs and felt it was her bounden duty to keep us all out of hell.

She'd commence by asking which mystery matched the day in question. We never knew, and would turn our mute faces towards her like a row of innocent pansies. Then she'd be off on a good five-minute's rant concerning our lack of religious knowledge.

Father would have taken up a comfortable kneeling position: arse in the air, elbows bogged in the cracked depression of that couch. He'd rouse himself — the hair, released from the restraining hat, standing up like a rooster's comb — and add helpfully: 'Aye, thir larnin' nothin' at that school, atall, atall.'

Truth be told we learned little else at that school. But we knew better than to present the case for the defence at that juncture, our sense of self-preservation being as keen as a hunted stag's.

When we finally got going, my mother would lead like a hare out of a trap. The rosary itself was a protracted ramble through the solemn terrain of 'decades', martyrs and saints. When this portion was exhausted, my father would already be hastening up the inside track with a non-stop version of the litany. His rapid delivery rivalled that of a southern Baptist preacher. 'Pray for us, pray for us, pray for us' we'd chorus in unthinking unison.

And it wasn't over yet. A raft of saints was implored to get various souls in or out of purgatory. Well, not exactly 'in' perhaps, but that's how it sounded sometimes to me. My mother had a list of names she routinely ticked off: those she obviously considered not quite fit to enjoy, just yet, the blissful reward of heaven. There was Aunt Jane, Great-aunt Mary, Uncle Willie, Great-aunt Mary Maggie, Great-aunt Biddy, Grandma Aggie Anne, Uncle Joe Paddy John, Aunt Minnie and — last but not least — Big Frenkie.

There was always a 'Big Frenkie' lurking in my childhood. If he wasn't being prayed for, he was being talked about. I imagined the phantom Frenkie in stout, black coat and hat, moving slowly and ponderously with the aid of a shiny Malacca-cane. I wondered idly what he'd done to be the subject of such supplication and talk, but I never got to know. As a child you knew not to ask questions about things or people that didn't concern you.

Consequently I locked in and bottled up all inquiry. Silence seemed safest. We all became expert at hiding our true feelings; we were like little impoverished automatons, existing in a hard-edged world of cause and brutal effect. On reaching adulthood I found that speaking up for myself was a difficult art to master. Harder still was learning to place any value on that which I had to say. I had so much to unlearn.

Great-aunt Rose and the Goat

As the gloom of winter gave way to spring, our journeys to and from school would become more tolerable. Progress home was slow as we dawdled by the hedgerows, plucking and examining anything of interest. We also understood the respite our weary mother enjoyed in our absence, and were in no hurry to even *glimpse* the dismissive face of father. So we trudged together, my two brothers in front and me trailing behind with my classmate Marie.

Marie was tall and kind and smart. Her face was stippled with a mass of orange freckles and crowned with a shock of russet hair that sprang out furiously from her head. With Marie I plundered the hedges for primroses or bluebells to carry home to mother, ignoring the objection of briars and nettles that tried to frustrate my trespass. And even if sometimes I did end up with the scratches and stings of my endeavours, it was worth all the pain, just to see my mother smile, which was all my heart desired.

There was something special about those sunlit journeys, as we lingered on the hot road, when the wind held its breath and the bees buzzed alongside us. The sun seemed hotter then: a glorious, golden gasp that caught the opulence of nature and held it close for my inspection. I saw it all with the clarity of an optometrist inspecting an iris. So close to everything at three foot ten.

The boys would amble on ahead, getting farther and farther away, pivoting round from time to time to urge me on. I'd see them whirling and shouting, but I was too engrossed, and they'd give up; the shouts of protest dying in the act of their turning back to the road.

As the days grew hotter we plodded and sweated under the cumbersome weight of schoolbags. We'd often heave them off and sit by the sunstruck roadside, eyes intent on the bubbling tar. Few cars or mortals plied the roads in those days so we had the country lanes to ourselves. The density of that reflected silence was ours as well:

> Absence with absence makes a travelling angle,
> And pressure of the sun
> In silence sleeps like equiloaded scales.

That silence was broken only sporadically by birdcalls and the needling hum of a tractor. The fields marked our progress, and throughout the year we marked theirs, from glossy upheavals of winter soil to calming intervals of green. The swathes of ripened corn in summer gladdened our hearts most of all; the golden prize of the long holiday was finally within reach.

Occasionally we'd be delayed by a strapping lady on a bike, grey hair standing on end and a navy-blue raincoat billowing out in concert with the breeze. We'd hear her approach, her breath coming out in great gusts of effort as she laboured up the hill behind us. We were a little afraid of her, so none of us dared look round until she spoke. Then she'd heave herself off the mighty conveyance and continue on foot beside us, wheeling the bike as she talked.

Mary Catherine was a pious lady who always enquired as to how we were, and assured us with breathy conviction that whatever day she happened upon us was the feast-day of a favourite saint.

She invariably had an oilcloth shopping bag, patterned with red and grey diamonds, swinging from the handlebars. When she had finished her spiel, she would hoke in it for a few moments while we waited expectantly, and produce a crumpled bag of brandy-balls. We were then each rewarded for our patience and indulgence.

There were many Mary Catherines in those days: rural women who, without the distraction of a husband and children, could devote their time to venerating the Sacred Heart and marking off the feast-days of saints on calendars. When I now consider my mother's demanding life, answering everyone's needs but her own, I realise how much more fortunate those single ladies surely were.

Yet Mary Catherine was gregarious in her own way. There were dwellings I passed on those journeys that had the power to intrigue and entice me: whitewashed hovels at the end of winding lanes that willed me to stop and look for signs of life. They were inhabited by strange, solitary individuals who, I suspect, lived on windfalls and tins of corned beef. These people were generally ignored by the community because they had not married and had children.

One such house belonged to an eccentric named Jamie Frank, a bachelor who wore a cap way back on his head and seemed to exist in a mysterious, interior world. When we'd meet him on the road he was barely aware of us, so engrossed was he with his own inner dialogue.

Sometimes when we'd pass his house we'd see him unhook the half-door and emerge, bearing a lidless teapot to empty on the dung-hill. He had the queerest walk; his pelvis jutting out, legs straying way in front, with head and shoulders lagging behind, like some sort of ambulant chair. Jamie never seemed to have company. Unlike Mary Catherine he hadn't found the need to call on the friendship or protection of saints; that protracted discourse with the self seemed to serve him just as well.

He usually kept a goat tethered to a post in one of his fields and one day, in an uncharacteristic act of delinquency, we stopped to hurl pebbles and abuse at the beast. It bucked and jumped in an agitated frenzy while we stood about, laughing and jeering at its wild antics. We were confident, you see, that the sturdy rope would protect us from all harm.

We were wrong. To our sheer astonishment and fright the animal broke free and hurtled towards us over the field, head down, avenging horns held low. We ran, yelling and screaming for dear life as the goat gained on us. We had no option but to dive into the yard of our Great-aunt Rose.

Old Rose was my father's reclusive aunt. She 'couldn't be doing' with noisome children, so you didn't bother her unless it was a real emergency. In my memory she is for ever ancient: a feeble dry stick with a crooked back, dressed always in black. Her rheumy eyes and dismal face had spent so much time judging the actions of others that she'd forgotten how to live herself. We were afraid of her, there was no doubt, but that fateful day we were forced to make a desperate decision; it was either Aunt Rose or the goat's revenge. We cried out for her help.

She hobbled out when she heard the racket, and chased the brute away with a few whacks of her knobbly blackthorn stick. She was never without that stick; it seemed like a natural extension of her arm. The danger past, she beckoned us into her gloomy lair.

And so we entered a cottage strewn with the detritus of decades gone: every surface furred with dust, the walls smoked yellow, the cobwebbed cornered windows; all was pervaded by the smell of smouldering turf and stewing tea, forgotten milk and bread. In short, the house reeked of a life in decay. We timidly sat down on a worn couch, the tumult of our narrow escape pulsing in us, and watched her make the tea she knew would calm us.

I remember the kitchen in the same way you'd recall a memorable visit to a museum in a foreign city. You take account of things because you know with near-certainty that the experience is unlikely to be repeated. Fear also has a habit of sharpening our recollection of things we'd prefer to forget.

Aunt Rose's kitchen was the wicked witch's den of fairytale. The soot-caked kettle hung over the hearth, boiling itself into a frenzy, and her black cat sat on guard to one side of it. When its mistress unhooked the kettle to wet the tea it roused itself and stretched, before padding to the door. We were motioned to the table with a curt nod and dumbly watched her fill the cups. It was easy to see she was not used to entertaining or being with children; this new experience put her out. I watched the rivulets of blue veins on the withered hand swelling with the effort of gripping the teapot. A plate of biscuits and ginger cake materialised from a deep drawer in a glass case and trembled their way to where we sat in the greenish glow of the recessed window. Shyly, we proceeded to eat.

I was frightened of Aunt Rose. We all were. I imagined that if the dead came back to earth they would probably look like her: the skin cracked and shrunken, the yellowed, joyless eyes and lipless mouth, the crooked body swathed in black. (I could not have known it then as I sat in the silence and the gloom, but before long those musings would come back to haunt me.)

After these quivering exertions the old woman returned to the stool by the hearth and composed herself. The stick was propped back in the corner and the shawl tightened about the bent back. These trusted gestures steadied her as she contemplated the flickering embers and the weight of our intrusion. I wonder what thoughts she had then and can only conclude that she looked on us as a nuisance she could well have done without. We munched the cake and biscuits and drank our tea in a conspiracy of silence, savouring this unexpected treat, wondering all the while about the charging goat that had driven us to her door.

This one incident jangled the rhythm of those days of habit. We'd steal past the billy-goat after that; one movement from it was enough to send us fleeing.

Normally I left Marie at her gate to the yelps of her excited Jack Russell. I'd continue over the Forgetown bridge, rounding McCrystal's corner and going down the lane. More often than not I'd be clutching the sweaty stems of the wildflowers I'd picked for mother, the emblems of my love for her.

When I look back, I see those reasons for dalliance — Jamie Frank, Mary Catherine, old Rose — as jerky images on an old-fashioned cinema screen. I hear the sluggish whirr of the reel and see the blend of motes and smoke in the steady beam of the projector's light. In my imagination Jamie becomes the silent poisoner, carrying the guilty evidence of his crime to the dump in that lidless teapot. Mary Catherine is the breathless angel gliding up that hill to enfold us in her wings, and Great-aunt Rose is the wicked witch hobbling out to censure us with her arid heart and accusing eye.

They're all gone now, to another place: all those mysterious people, the ones who passed their days largely ignored, trapped in those desolate shacks, flooded with loneliness, with only the ticking clock and crackling fire for company.

I did not understand loneliness then. These people were regarded as misfits to be feared, but now I realise

that at some point in their lives they had, for whatever
reason, taken the wrong turn, had wandered off that
main road which buzzed with life, where maidens sang
and children danced, where the birds and banter flew —
and had somehow lost their way. The saddest part,
however, is that no one in the community made the
effort to go in search of them and gently guide them back
to that sun-filled road.

Lipstick, Glamour and Death

In 1968 our house underwent a renaissance. An
extension was added, giving us the luxury of another
toilet, kitchen and bedroom. This last was an important
development for me. At night-time I no longer was the
filling in the sandwich; we had an extra bed.

My mother turned my old bedroom into what she
termed 'the parlour'. She even managed to prise a carpet
(brown; it wouldn't show the dirt) and a vinyl, three-
piece suite out of my father. For him it was a bold
extravagance; for her it was a victory.

The 'good room', as it was called, was only used on very
special occasions, and one of those occasions was when
the 'Yankees' came visiting.

Isa was the sister of a neighbour. She lived in Canada
and, faithfully every summer, she and her daughter
Regina travelled those thousands of miles to visit her
brother Sam and his infirm wife in Draperstown. They
were always referred to as the Yankees, my parents
believing that Canada and the United States were one
and the same.

The only time our house got a real seeing-to was
several weeks before their arrival. Windows were painted
and walls papered; my mother scrubbed, and shouted
with more vigour than ever, bellowing out commands
that nearly shook the house. In the interests of parsimony
and peace, the job of painting fell to my sister Rosaleen
and me. Mother knew from past experience not to ask

father, since anything he did inside the house was 'dear bought', as she put it. This meant that he complained so much before, during and after the execution of a given task that he nearly drove her 'mental'.

So we girls would go into action with the white gloss, tackling it with all the precision of a drunk in a lavatory. We strayed madly onto windowpanes, dribbled onto skirtings and floors, even coating the odd cockroach or insect that had the misfortune to blunder into the path of our reckless brushes. Mother seemed not to notice these mishaps; in fact she was so proud of our efforts that she'd send us to a straitened neighbour or myopic uncle to wreak the same havoc there.

We sang and slobbered away with our brushes in those other houses, knowing that no matter how careless our application was it probably wouldn't be noticed. We also reasoned that our results would definitely be an improvement on what was there before. But perhaps the greatest incentive for our insouciance was that the stingy relative never paid us in coin; the paltry reward was often a mug of tepid tea and a stale bun.

There was exuberance in the air at the thought of the Yankees' arrival, not least because the humble fare in the cupboard would be replaced with an assortment of cakes and buns which our impoverished palates knew were bound to come our way at some stage.

At the sound of their car there was a flurry of anxiety and excitement that no other visitors to our house could invoke. They caused us to perform to a higher standard, and even our established routines were tossed overboard. One of these involved the non-use of the front door; it would be stiff and unyielding because Rosaleen and I had invariably painted it shut.

'Christ, there's the Yankees!' mother would yell to father. 'Get off your arse and get that front door open.'

As the car approached, my father would use all his might to try to prise the door open, putting his foot up on the jamb in desperation while mother stood berating him for not having performed this very necessary task sooner.

'It's always the same,' she'd continue, panicking now. 'Declerta God, leave everything to the last minute. You hadn't a damn thing to do except that, and you couldn't even manage that. My heart's a breakin'. I may give this place up!'

When the front door was finally freed, the back one, which was always open, would bang shut in revolt, making everything in the house tremble and flap. It seemed as though the arrival of the Yankees had the power to unsettle even the contents of the house.

Then came the moment we'd all been waiting for. There was a crunch on gravel and a flutter of chiffon and suddenly there they were in the parlour, my mother ushering them in in her slippery viscose frock and plastic sling-backs, my father in his Sunday suit. My parents looked shabby by comparison with Isa and Regina, unwittingly lending these dames a radiance they did not fully deserve.

The visitors were all elegance and grace: lean ladies with delicate wrists, who moved cautiously on precarious heels, and cared greatly about appearances. They carried powerful handbags and wore a great deal of asphyxiating scent. We had never seen such shoes before: glancing patent leather which barely covered their dainty feet, with buckles on the toes that glittered. The hair was blonde and wavy, their smooth untroubled faces painted and powdered and perfect. Regina was a younger reflection of her mother, and Isa held the elegant promise of what the daughter could become.

They would arrange themselves on chairs either side of the fireplace, like two exotic birds flanking the listless space. I'd hang shyly in the doorway, awed by the glinting jewellery that moved and winked as they talked. And boy could they talk! Streams of languorous syllables would issue from them all afternoon, the fine hands fluttering and straying in the air for added emphasis.

They inspired mother to gaiety and father to alien acts of chivalry: I'd see him getting up to replenish the flutes of sweet sherry and light the proffered cigarettes, which were as long as their stilettos. We children milled around, sneaking looks at the unfolding spectacle – a Hollywood drama right there in our living-room with the Yankees centre stage.

Tea was the high point of this production and mother would reluctantly leave the guests, to direct operations in the kitchen. She didn't trust us, you see, and with good cause: she was aware that, left in charge of all the fancy food, we were liable to lose control and wolf down the lot.

She needn't have worried, however; the ladies barely touched a thing. The symmetry of those figures had to be maintained; cheekbones and hand-span waists were forever their priorities.

Mother would wheel in the trolley to showers of obliging remonstration.

'Oh Gawd, Mary,' Regina would protest, 'you shouldn't have! How absolutely divine.'

'You've gone to sooooo much trouble,' Isa would say, 'and we're only slightly peckish. Well, just a morsel then; those teacakes look super.'

They'd linger over the morsels with absentminded ease, an art perfected through years of dizzy-making self-denial. And so the cake stand with its tier of buns and biscuits would remain like an offence between them, the sandwiches gradually curling up in defeat. And our eyes would widen at the prospect of all those yummy leftovers.

Before departure there was a photo opportunity on the front step. We stood in an awkward group, bashful in the scrutiny of the camera. And there they are: Isa and Regina forever conquering the lens, with their brilliant hold-it smiles and the confidence they knew was rightly theirs. When they left, their subtle energies went with them and the house returned to its drab old self. We could still, however, imagine those lilting voices and still smell the soft exudation of that scent.

As the car bore them away we'd dive onto the cake stand, and mother would unwrap the gifts the ladies had brought. There'd be a plate or ornament with the predictable maple leaf or Mountie. Over the years we accumulated a great deal of Canadian tat; it jostled for prominence on walls and shelves, growing with each successive visit.

Being an awkward teenager, I wanted to grow up very fast and be just like the Yankees. I imagined having a white mansion on a sun-drenched hill. Every year I would take off from it like an effortless swan and land in dear old Ireland to pay a visit to the humble folk. I wanted to feel those flimsy fabrics next to my skin and the danger of those stilettos on my feet; I wanted to lay claim to all that urgent beauty that had the power to fell envious women and halt men in their tracks, to have the ability to electrify atmospheres with my wit and charm, and manifest every kind of goodwill in everyone I met. I longed for that sculpted elegance, the diamonds and the scent, the glamour and polish that belonged to another world entirely.

There was no compromise with the Yankees. They caused such beautiful riots in my head and left lasting impressions. I felt no quandaries of faith where they were concerned. They were so unlike my mother and the other women I knew, those who slaved and gave to others because that was their function. These ladies relaxed and gave to themselves, and that was their triumph.

Isa's brother Sam was a Seventh-day Adventist. In Ulster back then it was important to know a person's religion — more important, in fact, than knowing their name. People were either 'our sort', meaning Catholic, or the 'other sort', meaning Protestant. Sadly little has changed in this regard.

Master Robert claimed that he could guess a person's persuasion just by looking at them. It was a bizarre idea, coming as it did from an adult who appeared to be in possession of a fully functioning cerebral cortex. He'd say: 'I saw an odd-lookin' individual in the town today. He had the look of a Protestant about him.' And nobody thought to question the veracity of such a wild assertion. Such innocuous comments, foolish as they might have seemed at the time, all served to harden the cement that built the walls of division in Ulster.

Our neighbour Sam, with his Seventh-day Adventism and not belonging to a mainstream Protestant denomination, bucked the trend slightly; nobody quite knew where to place him. So he was put in a 'harmless cretur' box, along with the Quakers, Mormons and Jehovah's Witnesses.

The main tenet of Adventism is the belief that the second coming of Jesus Christ is imminent. Sam believed it, and his goodness was a reflection of that readying conviction. He worked the land, treated others well and cared for his sick wife, all without complaint.

He was a tall, rangy man with a shiny bald head and a wart between his eyebrows which moved up and down as he talked. Often, when his chores were done, he'd drop in for the obligatory tea and talk. When Sam sat down on our couch he resembled a collapsed deckchair, reclining on his backbone, knees scissored wide in front, arms strung across his chest, with only the head in motion, roving around for that essential eye contact as he chatted.

Not surprisingly, he shared his sister Isa's enthusiasm for the prattle. He'd speed in and out of subjects, giving loud opinions on everything. He'd brake briefly for my mother's feeble additions of 'You don't say, Sam', 'Away a that' or 'Are you sure now?' And then he'd be off again, gritting his lines with his own brand of swear-words — 'heck' and 'dang' and 'gee' — each calculated not to offend the Lord. Being neither Prod nor Taig he wisely steered clear of politics at all costs, seeing only shattered friendships and the dangerous glint of wreckage up ahead if that road were taken. And all the while he talked, mother's offerings would lie ignored, the tea going cold, the scone untouched.

His days began and ended with his two loves: his land and his wife. The land was his livelihood: the farm. His wife, disabled, unable to get about, meant that Sam had as much work inside the house as out.

I never met Anna but imagined a restive soul trapped in a wheelchair, compensating for the scourge of useless legs by reading, knitting, and creating. Every Christmas we received a card which she had lovingly made with tissue and lace; inside, the greetings of the season were rendered in a shaky hand. Sam would bring us the customary cake and a pot of his home-made jam. These gifts were so caringly created and all had an air of thoughtfulness and sincerity about them; they came from naturally benevolent people.

Then, without warning, the unthinkable happened. Sam — loving husband, loyal neighbour and endless talker

— vanished, and there was consternation in the locality.

Farmers of that era — and indeed the same holds true today — were forced to live according to the limits of their routines, in synergy with their land, their livestock and fellow farmers. When someone stepped outside the paradigm it created a warp, a stasis. Sam's untimely disappearance caused just this: a temporary faltering of hearts and minds.

His brother flew in from Toronto, leaving Isa to grieve, and the hunt got under way. For days the neighbours searched the surrounding countryside. They looked in sheds and trawled the rivers, but their efforts went unrewarded and everyone was left further perplexed. In our rambling rosaries we asked for Sam's safe return and — as the days collapsed into weeks and then months and the mystery deepened — we prayed for his heartbroken sister Isa so far, far away, enduring all that bafflement and despair.

Nine months later the agony of our not knowing was over. Sam's body, weighted with concrete, was recovered from a lake outside Draperstown. He'd been murdered by bank robbers whom he'd happened across in one of his barns. His threat to inform the authorities had betrayed him, and precipitated the end of the principled, decent man that he was.

With his passing, the Yankees withdrew. They could never 'come home' again. And their absence left a dull and empty present. I was so sad. All that former glamour and elegance had died along with Isa's brother.

When I think of Sam now I see him relaxing on that couch, the engine of his discourse forever running. I see my mother hovering in attendance with the tea. And I muse at the irony of how his speech could have betrayed him, and how his honesty could hasten such a brutal exit from all of our lives.

A Port of Dreams

In my childhood Sundays to me meant boredom. They seemed to be such listless days, hung like hammocks between the bustle of Saturdays and Mondays. Weekends meant release from torturous school but, if Sunday mass meant the preface of confession — and every three weeks it did — then the imminence of that ordeal tightened all my thoughts into a great ball of panic. My mother was a diligent auditor of our souls, and if she said you had to go, 'attending to your duties', as she called it, then there was no escape.

As Father Monacle, our confessor, ripened with the years, so his brain seemed to take on a worrying life of its own. He frequently nullified the solemnity of the confessional by repeating your list of sins out loud for the benefit of waiting penitents.

The disturbing part of all this was his unpredictability. Sometimes he'd repeat only one or two of your sins; at other times, if you were really lucky, none at all. But there were those unfortunate moments when he'd blast out the whole, shameful lot.

And not only that. If you'd really shocked him he was likely, as an afterthought, to stick his head out of the cubicle and demand that you go 'right up to the altar' to say your lengthy penance. I had already experienced this very embarrassment by the age of seven. It seemed that children and adults were all equal sinners in the eyes of the good father.

Naturally, having to endure this humiliation took its toll. Adults would push their hapless offspring into the box first — to test the waters, so to speak. Father Monacle would start his admonishings, each word highly amplified.

'Don't *ever* be stealing chocolate biscuits!' he'd thunder. 'Don't *ever* take the name of the Lord thy God in vain.'

You could sense a degree of fearful editing going on in the assembled row of heads.

Miss Collins, the local blatherskite, seemed always to be present, taking up a prime position near the box. My mother claimed this was more to do with nosiness than piety, which was probably correct. After all, who needed to forage among 'unreliable villagers' when Father Monacle could provide you with an amplified monologue via the confessional every Saturday evening?

Public embarrassment aside, when you came through this wall of fire the liberation felt like a Damascene conversion. I'd go home elated, get scrubbed and put to bed, to lie there in the dark, contemplating my shriven state and wondering if this sensation of holiness was what Miss McKeague had meant by 'being in a state of grace'.

Mass held little meaning for me when I was a child. During those rambling sermons, when the adults dozed off, I'd daydream that I was a glamorous singer in a band. Every Sunday I performed the chart-toppers of the hit parade — until the priest's voice woke me up with the Declaration of Faith.

Mass was an effortless affair, except when it came to receiving Communion. The bolt to the altar was fine; it was the return journey that presented difficulties; I'd sometimes lose my way and be unable to find my seat again.

Using ladies' hats as markers was not dependable because sometimes the owner of a hat could lose her place too. I tried using the Stations of the Cross as guides, but all that looking up at the paintings on the way down meant less concentration on where I was going, resulting in collisions with the oncoming 'traffic'. I ended up counting radiators; they didn't have the tendency to move.

Not surprisingly, the last thing I'd contemplate was the host I'd just received; the solemnity of the occasion never entered my head. When I finally regained the wretched seat in the correct pew, the race was on to swallow the host and get the prayers over and done with — in time to study that fetching hat of Mrs Convery's or my friend Doreen's new frock.

Did I gain any solace from these weekly trysts with God? The short answer is 'no'. These were perfunctory events which induced boredom and fear and gave me a heightened sense of my own inferiority. Sunday was God's day in name only.

My mother made a special effort on the Sabbath. There was the obligatory roast and — hallelujah! — a dessert: bowls of custard with a tinned pear or peach afloat in a deep lake of syrup.

After lunch, weakened by her labours, she would collapse into bed for an hour. Father, weakened by the thought that she was getting time off and, never one to be outdone, would retire to the couch, injuring it a little more. He'd scan the *Sunday Press* until all that lunch took its toll; the paper would rustle and droop, in concord with his snores.

Occasionally there were those luckless Sundays when there'd be an important GAA football match on the radio, a match that seemed interminable. Mícheál O'Hehir's volleying commentary was enough to drive a saint to drink. O'Hehir flung out the names and moves of players in high-pitched, wailing torrents. That familiar sound was enough to drive us children from the house.

In those flat interludes, with the sun shining and the chickens in the yard, I felt a bleak exultance. I was free to roam but at the same time aware of a paucity of feeling. I'd feel the pain of my mother's absence acutely. Her withdrawal for me meant boredom, longing, frustration, uneasiness; I missed her so much then, and I knew that these feelings would not disappear until she woke up again.

In the meantime I filled the absence with aimless wanderings over the territory I knew so well, and sought calm through jaded fictions. I'd chase the dog for no good reason; or wander into the barn and plunge my hands into the meal bin to feel the depth of the yielding grain.

Sometimes if I felt really impish I'd climb up on the tractor to make an imaginary journey. Gaining the tractor seat was its own reward. I loved to clutch the steering wheel with all my might and feel its tense refusal as I drove through the phantom fields. I'd close my eyes and throw my head back to bathe in the ardour of that steady heat of summer. In those minutes the world tilted and I saw oblivion, and heard the commonplace as some kind of melodious score, adrift and unconnected to me. Meditation in its infancy.

In the background the hens made their clucking speculations of the yard. From the house that rapid football commentary would slow from time to time, and belly out through the open door with triumphant declarations. 'And it's over the bar!' and 'It's a goal!' I'd hear my father raising a shout or oath depending on which team had scored.

All those simple amusements delayed me, rending up the time until mother would wake. It seemed that as she slept she withdrew all joy from me, leaving me lonely and aimless. I knew I had to wait until she rose before I could be returned to myself. She gave me purpose and meaning, made me realise what love was.

Those monotonous Sundays could sometimes free themselves and float up, to our delight, into the dreamy heavens, if only for one day each year. That was when we'd visit the seaside at Portstewart, and round off the day in Barry's amusement arcade in nearby Portrush. Both these heady destinations were referred to as 'The Port'. Being the deprived little mites that we were, we looked forward to this rare event with the same fervour we reserved for Christmas Day.

My mother would appoint the chosen Sunday well in advance and proceed to steer father unwaveringly towards it. She knew if she sprang it on him — say, only a week in advance — he'd be likely to come up with excuses for not going. The farm work, for instance, took precedence over any sort of family entertainment. Those two words were an oxymoron as far as father was concerned. But we needed him, and he was keenly aware of this; he was the only driver in the family and could exert a pernicious influence when it came to our mobility.

Mother always lamented the fact that he hadn't procured for her a driving licence when there was a free-for-all after the war. But perhaps it was for the best; being stressed most of the time, I doubt if she'd have made a good driver. Still, she used this negligence as a stick to beat him with whenever he refused to take her somewhere.

The outing always followed the same pattern. After mass and lunch we children would line up on the sofa, and wait while mother did her face: a lick of powder, lipstick and a dab of Coty scent. Meanwhile father was in the bathroom, engaged in the elaborate ritual of sleeking down his hair with the aid of water, Brylcreem and a comb; without the camouflaging hat this was a 'botheration', and we knew it. So we sat mutely on the couch, staring at the rhombus of sunlight moving slowly across the floor, wondering when we could get moving. No one knew better than we did that precious time was passing, but we didn't dare tell him to get a move on. The six of us lingered in the constricted silence and waited, praying that father's tense grooming formality might succeed, because if it didn't he could get in a mood and decide we weren't going 'atall, atall'.

Finally: all of us out the door and into the car, at first the Ford Popular and later a Ford Cortina (always a Ford; father rigorously resisted too much change) and we'd trundle off, doing an average of 40mph, mostly in third gear.

None of us enjoyed this journey. Apart from having to contend with the desperate drone of an underworked gearbox, we'd have to suffer the smoke from father's Woodbines; he insisted on all windows remaining closed, no matter how warm the day. So we'd sit in silent mutiny in the heat and sweat and smoke, suffering slow asphyxiation, knowing that if we dared complain he was liable to turn back and snatch our dream away. This being our only outing in the whole year, we could never risk jeopardising it. Instead I'd alleviate my discomfort with healing fantasies. As the fields and cluttered towns revealed themselves and receded outside the car window, I'd imagine feeling the hot sand between my toes and the waves before me: the rewards to come.

Portstewart is a beautiful, timeless town with a row of dwellings, shops and cafés facing by turns the vigour and calm of the Atlantic. A Dominican college to the west juts out onto a balcony of rock, overlooking with a lofty grace the sweep of sand and sea below. The generous strand is nearly three miles long; to us it seemed to stretch to the other end of the world. For the denizens of north Ulster back then this place represented a soothing release from the stresses of life; for us children it was pure paradise.

The climax of that tedious journey brought us release from the suffering of the car, and gave us the prize of that longed-for beach. Our little legs would have grown stiff and could barely take our weight as we tumbled out. Mother had kitted us out with swimming costumes; we young ladies each had a ruched one-piece in a fetching shade of blue or pink — and each one probably part of a 'buy one, get one free' promotion. She herself had a rather overstated one but in a similar style. The boys had their trunks, and father — ever the party-pooper — had no swimming gear at all, since he refused to take part in such frivolity. To him the whole excursion was a blatant waste of time. While we all had fun he'd sit in the car reading the newspaper.

Changing at the beach always presented difficulties, not least because there were no facilities and we didn't have a windbreak. So we'd all scramble up behind the sand dunes to undress.

Mother, being more worldly-wise than the rest of us, would keep a weather eye open for the ubiquitous peeping toms. On spotting one she'd fire off a volley of choice expletives. We never actually saw anyone but were assured that the 'dirty oul' frigger' had been out there none the less. I often wondered what he'd been looking for. I had the idea that every year it was the same man spying on us and was puzzled as to how he always managed to know the precise day and hour of our arrival. Mother claimed that the 'dirty oul' frigger' was everywhere and had eyes in the back of his head; so I'd struggle fearfully out of my dress and into my swimsuit knowing that no matter what I did, the brute could still see me. ...

The sea beckoned. We'd dash into the breakers and spend ages wading and splashing with delight. I gloried in the dynamic otherness of that buoyant world, and wished to remain in it for ever. But sadly the time would come for my farewell and I'd be dragged, kicking and screaming, from its shores.

After all that excitement came the picnic. Father was depressingly tight-fisted and would rather have undergone rectal surgery without anaesthetic than pay for us in a restaurant. So mother would spread a bath-towel on the sand and decant the contents of a large shopping bag. The lighting of the Primus stove was left to father and we'd all stand well back for the ceremony. Over his lifetime he'd perfected the art of making the simplest task look like a murderous assignment. Mother often ended up doing things herself rather than ask him because with each performance there was the petulant aftermath. When it came to the wretched stove, however, she was lost. She didn't know how to assemble it, and had neither the time nor inclination to learn, having enough to be getting on with.

We all stood well back for the lighting of the stove, hoping it would succeed and not blow up in his face because then there'd be hell to pay. With each failed attempt and spent match, father's face would grow longer and our hopes shorter. But it usually worked out. With the task accomplished, the parents drank their tea and we had warm milk or a cup of orange squash that had been diluted with such an alarming proportion of water that there was no discernible orange to speak of.

My mother could stretch the life out of food and drink until it begged for mercy. A single, humble tomato could sliver its way around an entire loaf; the salad cream bottle, on nearing expiry, would be watered and shaken vigorously to dislodge the last drop. She could have given Speke and Burton some useful hints on food rationing before they braved the deprivations of Africa.

Tomato and egg sandwiches did not travel well, as I recall, especially not in the boiling-hot boot of a Ford Popular. They'd emerge from their plastic bag well past their die-by date, just yearning to be squeezed into soggy balls and fired into the ocean. We didn't dare do such a thing, of course, the consequences being unimaginable; besides we were so hungry we'd have eaten anything. Wordlessly, we consumed the fare — sometimes with 'helpful' dustings of breeze-blown sand — because there was nothing else.

After the tea and sea it was off to Barry's, the amusement arcade in Portrush. We'd clamber into the car and trundle off on the two-mile journey to this second paradise. To us Portrush was synonymous with Barry's. We didn't see much more of the town itself; father claimed it was a 'black hole anyway', by which he meant it was full of Protestants, and for him that was good enough reason to shun it.

Getting us into Barry's was no problem — we'd race inside like prize sprinters — but getting us out again was a nightmare of tears, tantrums and much dragging of feet. We couldn't get enough of those moronic merry-go-rounds, sitting astride plastic ponies with mother urging us to 'hold on tight'.

Afterwards came the dodgems, the ghost train and big dipper. Sometimes on that stomach-lurching circuit those soggy sandwiches would take their revenge. We were denied nothing then. My mother reasoned, naively, that we could get too much of a good thing, and that if we had a go on everything we'd get so fed up we'd leave without a fuss. It rarely happened though. She had to resort to cajoling us with sweets of every description and the promise of ice cream in Morelli's café back in Portstewart. The bribe of ice cream always worked.

We'd drift along the promenade, licking the dripping ice-cream cones. In those golden moments we really did feel we'd died and gone to Miss McKeague's heaven.

Father would need his treat too. Before departing we'd follow him into a dingy pub – always the same one: The Slippery Eel on the promenade – and there he'd reward himself with a whiskey and a pint of Guinness. 'The Eel' seemed to be staffed by the same people and frequented by the same patrons year after year.

True to form, father would examine the bar counter with his seasoned carpenter's eye and give it a right good shake. Mother would note these disquieting indications, and shout out the order to distract him. 'God,' she'd whisper between gritted teeth, 'you could take that man nowhere. Let you down a bagful, so he would.' She was well used to his ways by then.

We were always served by the same barman: fat, tattooed forearms; face like a lump of Play-Doh pummelled by a child throwing a fit; purple parsnip nose. He wore a tight tee shirt which gave him a rather unflattering silhouette. He shuffled his feet, mumbled his words, and brought us our drinks on a dented tray which had no doubt doubled as an instrument of defence and combat during the occasional Saturday night brawl.

When we went to the toilet the floorboards shuddered. When a car whizzed past the window the drink in our glasses shivered. We got Fanta orange and mother had a Babycham, served in what looked like a glass saucer on a stem. With each sip her cheeks would go pink and she'd smile more. She'd frequently end up having a chat with the same woman every year: a middle-aged lady with a recent perm and red ears. Father would become more voluble, engaging some cap-and-braces wearer at the bar, who'd swerve with delirious uncertainty through a range of topics he knew little about. Those wise words of Lord Halifax come to mind now: 'Most men make little use of their speech than to give evidence against their own understanding.' And that surely went for father as well.

And we children, having finished the Fanta with lightning speed, with the adults occupied and our day at an end, would quest about for further amusement. Since we were forbidden to move from the table, its surface became the focus of our ennui: we'd lever off sections of Formica with bored fingers and stuff the evidence of our vandalism down the crack of the vinyl sofa seat. When the adults had finally finished and father was on his feet he'd look at the table and remark: 'God that Formica doesn't stand the times atall, atall. Nothing but a load of oul' British rubbish.' And the barman would sigh heavily, shoot smoke from his purple nose and counter: 'Aye, it's the bloody sun that does it, so it does ... curls it up like ... need tae get a lock of curtains, so I would.' With that we'd traipse out, experiencing the rare delight of having put one over on the adults.

We slept most of the way home, reliving in our dreams the pleasures of the day, our joy tempered by the thought that we'd have to wait a whole year before we could do it all again.

In childhood I climbed metaphorical mountains. Each year the terrain got harder and the ascent steeper. That one day by the seaside was the ledge on which I rested. Yet all the same it seemed that that one, red-letter, day repaid all the unnumbered days of sadness.

Bombs and Motorbikes

In 1970 the monster of political violence that would slaughter and slash its way across Northern Ireland for the next three turbulent decades was beginning to rumble and stir itself to life.

The so-called 'Troubles' began in 1967 with the formation of the Northern Ireland Civil Rights Association (NICRA). The movement called for equality for the nationalist population, among other things campaigning for the right of every person to have a vote, an end to discrimination in employment, and the need for a fairer system by which houses were allocated. Catholics had been denied these basic rights for decades within the one-party Unionist state, under governments that represented only the interests of the majority, Protestant, population.

To the outside observer this might have seemed a gross injustice that needed to be addressed. The Unionist people, however, for whatever reason, chose to believe that the NICRA was merely a front for the Irish Republican Army, whose goal was a united Ireland. Never mind that the IRA was almost non-existent at the time.

The more militant among the Unionists therefore felt justified in attacking any civil rights marches that took place. The thugs were supported by the mainly Protestant police force, the Royal Ulster Constabulary, who were supposed to be keeping law and order and protecting the demonstrators.

One such march in 1969 proved beyond doubt whose side the authorities were on. I watched the television footage of peaceful marchers – both men and women, Protestant and Catholic – being attacked by the RUC at Burntollet Bridge near Derry city. I did not know then that this event would mark the point at which the Troubles went from being primarily a civil rights issue to a return to a more savage time, one in which religion and national identity were paramount. I could not have understood as I innocently watched the batons and bricks rain down – as my father swore and my mother crossed herself – that this outrage would lead to more than 30 years of conflict and the deaths of over 3,000 people. Burntollet had picked open the scab of tribal hatred so that the blood of intolerance could gush forth again.

It was Belfast where the monster of sectarianism and bigotry thereafter chose to release most of its venom. Rarely having visited the city, my parents and country folk in general viewed Belfast as a war zone best avoided. The television brought the destruction close enough. Moreover each summer, usually on a Sunday, we received one of its citizens, a distant relative of my mother's: Mr Edward Bradley, affectionately known as Eddie.

In those phoneless days visitors could just appear out of the blue, which was rather distressing for mother, who could never keep a ready store of fancy food available for that unexpected guest, due to our skill at finding it. We'd discovered all the hiding places, so she'd simply given up trying.

Mother always prided herself on her acute sense of hearing. On certain Sundays, as we all sat sated round the dinner table, she'd announce that she could hear Eddie's bike in the distance. We'd all dash out to the yard and, sure enough, a couple of minutes later there he'd be, thundering down the lane on his big BSA motorcycle, the clouds of scree and dust billowing up extravagantly behind him.

The bike was a bizarre spectacle to us: a precariously dangerous machine that only the most daring and courageous could handle. When we saw Eddie hurtling down the lane he might as well have been a Martian and the bike a skyrocket.

We'd wait in suspense as he brought all that throbbing metal to a halt by the gable of the house, and watch in fascination as he performed the elaborate ritual of extricating himself from his biker's gear. Off came the bat-winged leather gloves, then the little bald head was freed from the helmet. Finally he'd swing a short leg over the rear of the machine with a pained expression that could only mean 'bloody sore arse' — and it's only now that I realise what BSA could have stood for.

Eddie was a crusty bachelor in his early fifties who could not relate to children. Yet I suspect that he secretly enjoyed all the attention he commanded in those moments when we stood around speechless, our eyes like saucers. He'd largely ignore us, not speaking until our parents appeared on the step. After handshakes and greetings he'd follow them into the house, creaking in his leathers, and we were left to inspect the bike. We smelt the petrol fumes and made faces in the reflecting belly of the tank, fighting for possession of the saddle as we took imaginary journeys with our very own *vroom-vroom* sound effects.

These yearly visits served Eddie's twin objectives of seeing mother and pursuing the salmon that teemed in the Moyola river. I say 'pursue' because, for all his fishing expeditions, Eddie never seemed to catch anything. He would squeak back to the house after three hours or so, empty-handed. We'd learn that he'd caught 'one or two wee tiddlers like', that he'd tossed back in again.

While he was engaged in this fruitless exercise, mother would be away at the shop frantically buying an assortment of 'sweet stuff' for his tea. There was no getting away from the fact that Eddie had a very sweet tooth; he had the belly and dentures to prove it. So a sugary mess – a dentist's nightmare – was laid on for his return. There were Mr Kipling's French Fancies, Battenburg cake, jam tarts, Swiss roll, chocolate biscuits, custard creams, chocolate eclairs, the whole gooey lot assembled for his 'highly refined' palate. I would have loved one tenth of what was on that table, but mother was adamant that nothing would be touched until our guest had had his share. She was unstinting when it came to Eddie; after all, he'd come a long distance on that dangerous contraption, from the great hell-hole that was Belfast, just to see her.

We children were exiled to the yard while he feasted and would take turns to go and sneak a look round the parlour door to see how he was faring. We lived in the vain hope that he'd leave a few morsels behind. He rarely did; maybe a half-eaten custard cream that his stomach had rejected in a final act of rebellion and good sense. We loved the 'Yankee' visits more than Eddie's, with very good reason.

After the binge he'd ease his ample little frame into a chair by the fire and place a lighted John Player in the corner of his mouth. There the cigarette remained, joggling up and down as he talked, the ash falling casually and unnoticed onto his lap. He'd sit there regaling the parents about the awful happenings in Belfast, his eyes watering and forehead pleating with the effort of his testimony.

Eddie drew the dreadful pictures and my parents coloured them in. They were astonished at his obvious skill in dodging the bullets and bombs on a daily basis. My father would wonder how he'd managed to survive thus far without a mark on him. Eddie put it all down to the speed of his legs and a keen sense of detecting danger, though when you looked at his fat belly and short legs you did question his ability to walk fast, let alone run.

His departure held for us as much fascination as his arrival. We all gathered in the yard to watch him get into the protective clothing. He now had difficulty buttoning the leather jacket. Then he'd don the helmet and gloves, and revert to the mysterious being from another world.

My parents' parting words included warnings. 'Look after yourself in that wild place,' mother would say, 'and safe home, Eddie.' And with that he'd trot with the bike a bit, before jumping astride it and away they'd go, farting blue smoke and playing merry hell with the gravel and dust. We'd remain standing in the yard to hear the last of that roaring farewell.

'God, that could be the last time we see wee Eddie,' my mother, ever the optimist, would say, 'what with all that bother in the city.'

Yet he'd be back the following year without fail, having survived the onslaughts to tell us yet more of his grisly tales. My brothers looked forward to Eddie's visits in the same way we sisters looked forward to seeing the Yankees. To them that motorbike was the embodiment of masculinity, just as those elegant stilettos were the epitome of womanhood for me.

Sadly, all good things come to an end; in the case of Eddie's visits the end came as abruptly as those of the Yankees. The circumstances were, however, far less traumatic.

It all started when two of my sisters landed jobs in the great city of Belfast and went to live there. They discovered to their bemusement that it was not the fearful war zone Eddie had painted. In fact they could live in relative safety. There was the occasional bomb in the city centre. There were also isolated pockets or flash-point areas where violence erupted more frequently, but you avoided those places if you could.

Eddie had also claimed that he worked as a civil servant in Stormont Castle. This had really impressed the parents, Stormont being the seat of the Unionist government.

For a wee Taig like Eddie from the Falls Road to actually get a job at the very heart of the Establishment was no mean feat. My mother claimed that it was a miracle in itself and proof — if proof were needed — that her humble relative could climb the career ladder without missing a step.

One fateful day mother decided to pay Eddie a surprise visit at his place of work. To her astonishment she bumped into him emerging from the ladies toilet, steering a trolley laden with cleaning agents and a mop bucket. The embarrassment of this unexpected meeting proved too much for poor Eddie, and sadly we never saw him or his mighty BSA again.

ONE FRIEND, MANY STRANGERS

Throughout the trials of raising us virtually single-handedly and putting up with the mood swings and demands of an uncaring husband, my mother attempted to achieve some sense of dignity and balance in her life. But it was extremely difficult. Father could sulk for hours over a trivial matter: at the dinner not being hot enough – even though he had delayed coming to the table when called. Whatever she cooked was never right; it was too hot, too cold, overcooked, underdone. 'You'd swear that man had been raised in Kensington Palace, so you would,' my mother used to complain to a neighbour.

His behaviour was that of a truculent child. When he was out doing the farm work, there was a tenuous kind of peace indoors, but on his return the air would darken and our talking cease. Whatever elation we had been experiencing we'd gather in again, and we'd trim our sails before the coming tempest.

Father did not like to see us happy; he found displays of happiness offensive. Consequently we learned to modify our behaviour to suit his moods. For him life was for enduring, not enjoying. In father's presence hope receded, intention died, ambition cracked. He liked to show the underside, forever turning up the fissures and the faults as if to say: Look, this is how you really are, all frayed and flawed just like me, so don't even try.

One day he came into the bedroom I shared with my sister Rosaleen and tore down all our posters. It had taken us quite a while to collect and display all our favourite pop stars, yet he could not afford us this very minor indulgence. We dared not ask why he'd done it. So we remained quiet while he vandalised our little treasures and cried silently when he'd gone.

He'd interrogate mother over the amount she'd spent on an outfit she'd bought. She therefore learned to adjust prices for his benefit in order to keep the peace. She knew from experience that honesty meant a sullen silence that could last for hours. Often she'd end up hiding her purchases rather than face the inquisition.

My mother had one ally during these trying years. She was something of a surrogate sister, and her nearest neighbour.

Helen lived across the road from us with her elderly parents in a big, pebbledashed house. She was the dutiful daughter to a possessive mother and father. Helen, like my mother, was rarely idle. She did not have children but she did have a farm which she managed by herself. In addition she was the cook, cleaner, carer, gardener — and did whatever other work demanded her attention in the course of a busy day.

For me she will be for ever 25, this being the age she was when the toddling me became aware of her. I have a photo of the teenage Helen. Her mother is seated and Helen, wearing a Fair Isle cardigan, is resting her hands on the older woman's shoulders, like two loving epaulettes. The women cannot bear the intrusive lens and gaze off with feigned interest at something out of frame. They were private individuals, not used to being the centre of attention: guarded, passive, unassuming.

Helen's appearance did not alter much with the years. She had curly auburn hair and wore harlequin glasses which made her look deceptively serious. She was all goodness and dependability, with a kind and gentle demeanour much like that of my teacher Miss McKeague. She was one of those rare adults I could connect with as a child. Her look and smile seemed to say: Yes, I know all about you: the pain and joy of all the stages you will go through: the present child, the future girl and — far off — the woman you'll one day become.

Helen was an only child, the product of a late marriage and thus hindered by over-protective parents. She was caught between a wish to marry and not wanting to desert them; this inner clash kept her bound and committed to their needs until they died. In her thirties she was finally free to marry, and she did so to a lovely man, at last experiencing the happiness that was her due. Now and then, when my parents had a day away, mother would entrust my two youngest brothers and me to Helen for safekeeping.

I loved Helen's house, a large mysterious place with many rooms, stairways and secret passages. There are certain features of it that will not fade. They stand out as familiar reference points in what was really a home from home; the polished boldness of the kitchen floor, with the same range and scrubbed table as mother's; the armchairs by the fire with the limp, crocheted cushions, where Helen's mother sat and knitted and her father smoked or dozed.

In the hall there was a hatstand with an oval mirror reflecting an effrontery of china and brass; several figurines and an ornamental kettle balanced precariously on its ledge, with an umbrella bucket by its side. Mother claimed that Helen could display all the frills and baubles she desired because she didn't have a 'clatter of youngsters' to go upsetting things, which was undoubtedly true. Part of my fascination for the house was bound up in this medley of curios and knick-knacks.

It was the parlour though that I loved the most. If it was raining we'd be put in there by the fire with a book or a jigsaw. Every five minutes Helen's apprehensive mum would look in with a host of concerned enquiries, her well-meant intrusions making us uneasy. She was not used to having children around. We were an unexpected luxury in her unchanging days.

The low-ceilinged parlour was a grand room and I felt special being part of it, like a decorous jewel that had been placed there to lend it a further polish. I remember that you stepped down into it because often I would forget and tumble in instead, causing Helen's mother a brief spasm of alarm. The only life in the still space was a roaring fire that made its blazing statement on even the hottest day. Two china spaniels kept guard on either side of the mantelpiece and a gilt-framed landscape hung above it. In front of the window stood a highly polished round table. On its gleaming surface Helen would spill out a puzzle and I'd sit for ages trying to solve the riddle of its scattered pieces.

In the corner of the room there was a china cabinet. The flames from the fire vivified a crowded display of teapots and silver, porcelain and glass. These were ancestral wedding gifts and sovereigns, pieces not intended for practical use but to be exhibited as proud reminders and evidence of past enthusiasms.

My mother didn't own one of these contemporary status symbols. Her humble wedding presents would not have run to filling a single shelf let alone a whole cabinet; besides, she was never allowed the money to 'throw away on such nonsense'. She blamed the lack on her spirited offspring, but that was not really the case. Helen's house held hoards of unbreakable beauty my poor mother could never aspire to: lengths of ribbon and delicate lace, lavender sachets in drawers of embroidered linen, crocheted place mats of deft needlepoint, all wrought by Helen's clever hand.

The main attraction for me was the flight of stairs. Going up them made me feel I was rising above myself. The twelve stairs in Helen's home ascended mysteriously and enticingly to a corner of paradise: her bedroom. When I'd hear her coming in from doing her chores I'd run out of the parlour and sit looking longingly up those stairs. She knew the signal well.

'Now,' she'd say, 'I wonder what you're lookin' up there for, Teen.'

And I'd always say: 'My face, Helen. I want my face pretty, Helen. Please, Helen, please.'

She'd smile and tease me with: 'But you *have* a pretty face, Teen, you wee rascal.'

She knew that compliments would not placate me and, without further ado, she'd take me by the hand, to lead me up to her room to be transformed.

Mother would surely have envied this room. It held a dazzling array of objects I'd never seen before. There were pictures in silver frames, biscuit tins stuffed with letters and old photos and, what arrested me the most: the jewellery and make-up, the mother-of-pearl hairbrushes and cut-glass bottles of scent that cluttered the dressing-table. Here was gathered together all the grandeur and glare of the accoutrement a women needs to amend God's lapses.

The wardrobe was stuffed with frocks, crinoline petticoats and pairs of white stilettos. At the weekend, when she went out with her fiancé, Helen would emerge from that bedroom a different woman; her hair brushed free, the nails and lips an urgent red; silver bangles crowding her wrist. The stiff, full skirt of her dress was as buoyant and generous as a ballroom dancer's. Gone was the farm worker in the old wellingtons and tattered overalls, and in her place stood a movie queen.

The highpoint of my day was my transformation before this altar to vanity. I'd sit up on her velvet stool before the mirror while Helen assisted me in the gaudy conversion of my face. First came the scarlet lipstick which she'd unsheath from the golden tube and help me hold steady. Then the shadow, which I could just about manage, stroked in splodges with a clumsy forefinger; after that a squirt of scent behind the ears and on the wrists.

The jewellery was next: strings of fake pearls and a sparkling, rose-shaped brooch that I adored. Then the bangles and a pair of earrings whose grip almost made my eyes water, but the pain was worth it just to see the lineaments of my plain little face changed so wonderfully. The nail polish was too demanding so Helen would put a tiny dot on each nail and help me down off the stool and into the finishing flourish: a pair of high heels. I was a princess then, a Yankee; with a few bold strokes I'd been restyled as one flashy lady indeed.

I'd clip-clop around for an hour or two, giving my brothers looks of jaded condescension, until all that beauty took its toll in straining legs and wounded earlobes and fading colour. At that stage, with the greatest reluctance, I'd give in and allow Helen to relieve me of my finery, standing forlornly while she went to work with a damp facecloth, stripping me back down to my colourless self. I often wept at this point, barely hearing her soothing words that promised we could do it all again very soon.

As compensation she'd sit me on the sun seat outside the parlour window and give me a shoebox of discarded wool and a pair of knitting needles. She always did the hard part of 'casting on' which I could never manage and start me on yet another multicoloured scarf; very soon the hurt of that earlier infraction was forgotten as I toiled with the needles, knitting out my frustrations.

Helen's life was not an easy one. Her ailing father hobbled around on crutches, the onset of rheumatism having retired him early, so all the back-breaking farm work fell on the shoulders of his only daughter. Mother said that Helen was doing the work of ten men, which was probably close enough to the truth. She not only kept more livestock than we did, but half her fields were under crops of all varieties.

Despite everything she never complained. She was a thoroughly decent woman who proved to be a crucial adjunct to my mother's otherwise barren social life. Whereas today's women swap the banalities of the current television soaps, mother and Helen swapped recipes and knitting patterns; their hands and heads were their creative strength. Activity beats passivity any day; it's what kept them both sane.

They confided in each other, these exchanges carrying them over the rocks and rapids of their lives. They both had awkward men to deal with. Helen's father was not a happy man; even as a child I could sense his severity. I suppose that trailing around those withered legs between crutches was hard, but the burden of that injustice was felt just as acutely by the two ministering angels at his side: his daughter and his wife.

Helen was a Presbyterian who took her faith seriously. The fact that she was my mother's closest friend says a lot about her courage and open-mindedness in a climate of religious zealotry and intolerance. She went to Sunday school, attended the Young Farmers Association dances and was a member of the Women's Institute.

Once a year the WI ran an outing — or rather a shopping expedition — to a city either within or beyond the province. Helen would often invite mother along and when I got a little older I was inveigled into accompanying her for moral support. These outings brought me inside the world of grown-up women and gave me my first taste of religious bigotry, albeit in a mild form. Mother and I were usually the only two Catholics on the excursion bus. I remember especially those trips to the town of Ayr in Scotland, not least because I was taken outside Ireland for the first time.

It was a lengthy journey — coach, ferry crossing and coach again — and we had an early start. The ladies, cheerful and animated, would assemble around 7am in the village square of Tobermore. There was a real buffet of beliefs in this congregation: Methodists, Baptists, and Presbyterians, both 'captive' and 'Free'.

This diversity has always made me think of our monolithic Catholicism as boring, all of us supping from the same doctrinal cup. At the same time, though, God is God, a singular and consistent deity, so why do we feel the need to take so many routes to His door?

It was clear that mother and I carried the wrong label, which made us outsiders in the eyes of the WI ladies. They showed a marked restraint in their greetings and chitchat. These ladies who carried Sunday service hymnals in their handbags and such evident disfavour in their hearts did not share Helen's candour and compassion it seemed. Looking back, I have to give credit to my mother who, vastly outnumbered by the 'other sort', was attempting the building of bridges across the religious divide at a time when such ideas had not yet entered the collective consciousness of Northern Ireland. Nowadays leaders of nationalist parties, following the example set by the illustrious John Hume, talk about the necessity of 'parity of esteem' between Catholics and Protestants if the political process in Northern Ireland is to have any hope of success. 'How can we move the process forward?' our politicians often ask. I feel proud that Helen and my mother were attempting to do exactly that even then, when there was no sign of a 'process' and not much hope of a 'forward' in sight.

The WI sorority were a well-rounded bunch. They were childbearing, cake-baking, husband-tending toilers, who like my mother were the overworked consorts of lesser men: farmers and tradesmen, with the odd doctor's wife thrown in to elevate the assembly. The wife of a professional man always stood out because she was usually leaner and richer and therefore more elegantly turned out than the rest.

The ladies' dress code created a showcase for synthetic fabric. At least poor mother felt comfortable with *that*. There were acrylic cardigans and polyester slacks, sometimes a Norman Lynton frock (designed for the fuller figure) with a boisterous splash of flowers and spots. The ladies' accessories harmonised the whole: the fake pearls and brooches worn high on neck and breast as a nod to Her Majesty; the plastic sandals and handbags in dependable, take-you-anywhere, go-with-everything beige.

There were other bags as well: carrier bags full of comestibles for the long journey. It seemed, too, that every half-hour the coach would make a comfort stop; it was as though the twin acts of satiating and 'titivating' could not be neglected in case some sort of irreparable injury resulted. So the driver would pull over and, after a prolonged tussle with bags and Tupperware, a silence would descend and the ladies would tuck in.

After the food, the toilets, involving a rather prolonged period of waiting; all that peeling down and rolling up of elasticated hosiery took its time. Then it was back on the bus for the interminable roll-call. Those ladies had allowed themselves to be so subsumed into the hegemony of their husbands that as well as forfeiting their surnames the first names had gone too. There was Mrs David Alcock, Mrs Ivan Baillor, Mrs Lester Paddock, and on and on it went. We could have been to Ayr and back twice over by the time this rigmarole was completed after every stop.

Mother could identify with our fellow travellers on an emotional level if not a religious one. Their bodies were like hers, swollen from giving birth and eating too much. Their once slender fingers now wore wedding rings sunken into flesh, the hallmark of unstinting service and union. They were encumbered by the choices they had made. Even though they attended different churches, they all sang from the same hymn sheet and genuflected at the patriarchal altar.

Those annual outings were usually to either Ballymena or Fermanagh, or perhaps to Lisburn; all good, secure seats of the Unionist ethic. For the WI ladies the diversionary coastal resort of Ayr was safe too. Scotland was the country from which their Protestant forebears had migrated, to plant and flourish in Ulster. They therefore felt safe amongst their own kinsfolk.

There were much more accessible and varied places to visit across the border in the south of Ireland, but to stray into the foreign Republic was never an option. I can hear them discussing this possibility:

'You mean you want us to walk among those Gaelic paddies and spen' time and money bolstering the economy of that Provo den? Are ye mental?'

'But we'd save a lot of travellin' time and ha' more time to dander round the shops if we went somewhere nearderhan.'

'Nonsense. I'd rather spen' a whole day on the bus than go near that hole. Sure it's full of clatts and you wouldn't get a decent bite anywhere. Give me good Ulster produce any day. At least y'know what yir gettin' and I'll tell ye something else, Mildred ... nivver trust a Taig. Thir throughother and lazy and they'd fight with thir ow' shadow, so they would. Sure look how thi've ruined our Ulster.'

And so to Ayr, which turned out to be as drab as any provincial town. It seemed we weren't very well rewarded after all that bus-ing and boating. There was the additional complication of a dialect no one could understand, since the Ayr folk mostly sounded like their hero Rabbie Burns, or wee Andy Stewart. We usually ended up using sign language in shops as our thick Ulster vowels and dialect brought looks of equal bewilderment from the natives.

After wading through the shops for an hour or two, we'd break for high tea at a family-run hotel. Generally I find that such establishments are not a good idea because they are usually staffed by the offspring of the owners, who do not share the parents' enthusiasm for success or profit.

So, under the glum gaze of these youngsters, we'd file into a room of refectory tables and sit waiting to be served. More often than not the fare was the reliable old salad — expedient, seasonal and therefore cheap — consisting of a few leaves of sad lettuce bedecked with a halved tomato, a quartered egg and a suspiciously shiny slice of ham. There'd be a complimentary glass of orange squash — or rather orange water, which smacked of mother's picnic formula: one part squash to 20 parts water. There was no alcohol in sight, it being considered the devil's buttermilk; on all those trips not even a glass of wine ever passed our lips.

The ladies never seemed to notice the shoddy quality, though, and would coo with delight when presented with this 'healthy display'.

They all seemed to be on diets — it was the main topic of conversation — and greeted the low-calorie fare with the triumphant-defeatist notion that by being 'good' with the main course they could 'sin' afterwards, free of guilt. Most eyes were on the sinful bowl of sherry trifle and fresh cream that invariably sat, wobbling and glistening, on the sideboard.

Losing weight was a good, gelling topic that helped mother ingratiate herself with her sisters. It seemed that she and everyone at the table was on the F-plan diet. Mrs Lester Paddock was 'very well reduced' and tangible proof of its efficacy, if any were needed.

So the ladies would discuss dieting with gusto, each trying vainly to recapture the figure of the carefree bride in the wedding album. But the fantasy would remain just that; without knowing it they'd pushed themselves out of the picture, to put husband and children first. For brief moments on the return journey I saw flashes of the girls they must have been. The ladies would let themselves go, waving at men as we passed through towns and collapsing in giggles when the men responded. They sang songs and clapped their hands, high on the oxygen of having been set free for the day.

Finally, after the return ferry crossing, when the bus drew to a halt in the village square, there were the menfolk: husbands or sons waiting in purring vehicles to take the women back home to their *real* lives; back to cook and to wash, make beds and clean, to toil under pictures of England's fair queen.

Leave-taking was a great orchestration of shouting and waving and arranging to meet again. There was always a bring-and-buy sale, or a guest tea or jumble sale at the parish hall to be getting on with.

These rare appointments with freedom and gaiety were what those women lived for. Those outings, simple and uneventful though they were, lifted their spirits, however fleetingly, into happiness.

The 1970 excursion did my mother a power of good. It was just as well, because not long after she'd need all the strength — both physical and spiritual — she could muster. Our home was to experience a truly bizarre and frightening episode.

The Haunting

There are certain things which defy logic. We journey through life so attuned to the realities of the material plane that we blind ourselves to the manifestations of the incorporeal. But sometimes the spectral universe clamours for our attention to such a degree that we are forced to acknowledge its reality. I was compelled to confront this reality when I turned eleven.

Up until then I had never thought much about death or dying, much less about ghosts or spirits. When a child I had listened to stories from the mouths of old-timers about wailing banshees and menacing fairies, and always been careful to vitiate the terrible endings with fingers stuck in ears.

Although I was aware of the existence of these ethereal visitors, they remained incomprehensible abstracts. They were as elusive as the heavenly firmament that I roamed in my dreams, or that piece of sky I tried to trap in my cupped hands as I lay on my back in the sunlit garden.

All my innocent musings were to undergo a dramatic shift in the autumn of 1970, and my notions of life, death and the hereafter would be altered for ever. Late one evening an extraordinary visitor arrived in our midst, unannounced and unrecognisable. It remained for six harrowing weeks, rupturing the calm, amber days and ripping through our senses with an urgency and vigour that is unforgettable.

The story begins with the waning of Great-aunt Rose, and that in turn was preceded by another occurrence: the raging goat that had driven us to her door on that hot May day. These things held the genesis of an awesome future event. For one fateful hour old Rose had been forced to exhibit unthinkable kindness; offering us tea and cake had stirred her heart and quelled our terror. It was the first and last time she'd shown such generosity of spirit towards us, and we were not to know that it came with a price. As I've remarked before, benevolence and compassion were not features of my father's forebears.

In late August that same year our great-aunt slipped while carrying turf from the shed, and the injuries she sustained put her into hospital for a time.

My mother saw the fall as a long overdue comeuppance for a selfish life. Old Rose barely countenanced mother's existence, despising her for having corrupted one of her nephews and having the gall to bring forth children as tangible evidence of that corruption.

But mother — always the forgiving, dutiful sort — offered to take care of her until she'd regained her strength. Uncle Robert didn't know how to; he knew how to take care of money, but not of people. His aunt Rose had quite a stash; the mean-spirited often do. Money, it seemed, was her very purpose in living. For Robert, the thought of getting his hands on it was what kept him attentive to her needs.

So the boys' bedroom was cleared to accommodate the patient and the parlour became their temporary sleeping quarters. However, despite mother's unstinting care and devotion, Great-aunt Rose never recovered from the fall; it had propagated the cancer that would release her from the bitter past and agonising present, and into the 'painful' future of the hereafter. She spent a month with us, after which Robert moved her to the guardianship of the nuns at the Nazareth House in Derry.

She died soon after. My mother received nothing for her trouble; the nuns were paid handsomely for theirs. Robert's attentiveness paid off as well. He received the bulk of her squirrelled-away £300,000 fortune.

The clergy fared handsomely too. It is a rather depressing feature of the miser's canon that he will seek reprieve from punishment in the next life by generously greasing the palms of God's representatives in this one. It seems that God takes on the role of the last great banker in paradise. Who knows how many monastery farms have expanded, or priestly purses have fattened, on the logic of this fallacy?

On 31 October, approximately six weeks after Rose's demise, my nine-year-old brother John was woken by the sound of a light tapping from under his bed. It was the same bed his dying great-aunt had lain in, and he shared it with his brother Mark. He wandered into mother's room and told her that he couldn't sleep. She listened, concluded that the tapping was caused by an agitated water pipe, and sent him back to bed. But the tapping persisted and, with Mark's help, mother and I dragged the mattress from the bed and into the kitchen. The boys eventually fell asleep there.

The following day, however, the tapping could still be heard, only this time it had travelled, and continued to travel: we heard it coming from various points on the floor of the boys' room. This disproved mother's noisy water-pipe theory.

With each passing day the frequency and volume of the eerie sound increased. After a week, when all efforts at a logical explanation were exhausted, the bed taken apart and reassembled, the floor inspected, the foundations checked, we were forced to come to the unnerving conclusion that we were dealing with a supernatural entity.

As a child, having to face this reality was extremely terrifying. It was a truth I would never fully have the measure of, or be able to banish from my thoughts. It was like witnessing a horror that had occurred within my field of vision, while I was innocently focusing on a beautiful landscape.

There were no ready answers to my questions because they lay outside the limits of human understanding. This was a malevolent invasion and it gripped me with a fear more terrible than anything I'd ever experienced. I thought I'd known dread in Father Monacle's confessional and Master Bradley's classroom. Such fears were nothing compared to this.

The growing terror inside me kept apace with 'its' progression. After a week it began hammering on the walls and floor of the boys' room; furniture would groan and the bed shake. Every nerve and sinew in us began to tighten in response to those awful sounds, only easing briefly when we thought they'd at last gone away. I don't know how many times we'd turn from the door to that room with tremulous hope.

'It's gone,' one of us would say without much conviction. 'Shush ... listen; it doesn't usually take this long. That's it. It's definitely gone.'

I can still feel the hope that flickered in me then and grew to a blaze of pathetic longing. We'd enter the boys' room and wait in the testing silence, in the calm before the storm, in the chill of that room. We'd wait, praying, hoping, standing stock-still, not daring to blink or swallow or breathe too deeply in case — just in case. But as sure as hell and heaven it would come: the thunderous communication from another place, and it would tear screams from every throat and precipitate a headlong dash, back into the terror we'd tried to escape from. It acted like some kind of demon doctor at a sickbed; at any given hour it would deliver a dose of fright and panic to keep us mindful of the fact that it had the power. We were the patients in need of healing, but the big question was: who or what had caused the contagion in the first place?

Mother went frantic. Her only recourse was to multiply and prolong the rosaries; we often said ten a day. The parish priest, Father O'Neill, came to listen to the noises, and said that prayer was the only weapon we had. He concluded that it was the soul of Great-aunt Rose. She was in torment in purgatory, he told us, and needed our invocations in order to be released. He got down on his knees and assured her of our continued devotion, beseeching her to be gone to her rest. But she refused his plea and continued to fill our sleepless nights with fresh assaults.

We noticed that the phenomenon seemed to follow John. He was the youngest of those of us who had supped at our great-aunt's table that fateful day. During that first incursion it had tapped its way from under the wardrobe at the far end of the bedroom, and settled under John's side of the bed.

We experimented with it. The oilcloth was lifted from the floor so as to dampen the sharpness of the raps, but the noise continued unabated, the volume shifting in consonance with the stone floor. We'd evidently angered it. Suddenly the tapping ceased and something altogether more horrifying replaced it. We heard the excruciating rasp of fingernails being dragged, sometimes rapidly, sometimes slowly, along the underside of the mattress.

Whenever John left the room the knocking, thumping and scratching would stop. Whenever he was laid on the bed it started up again; if one of us lay down beside him it quietened; when he was lifted free of the bed, it stopped. A crucifix placed on the bed would cause it to shake violently; when it was removed, the shaking ceased. All these variations in sound and movement demonstrated to us that the being had an uncanny sense of awareness. Sometimes when visitors called we'd have to turn up the volume on the TV to drown out the unearthly racket in the bedroom.

My parents viewed the menace as an aberration somehow brought on by the family, and therefore something to be mortally ashamed of – on a par with the ignominy of a daughter going out with a Protestant.

Such scruples also prevented us calling in the psychic detectives, experts who could throw authoritative light on the mystery. By the same token we couldn't have chequebook-toting journalists – and, God forbid, banner headlines in the local newspaper – or the prospect of a book perhaps and the sale of the film rights. William Peter Blatty wrote *The Exorcist* and Jay Anson *The Amityville Horror* (the latter since unmasked as a hoax), and there we were with the screenplay for *The Forgetown Phantom* being hammered out in our midst, blocked by mother's shame and father's ignorance. Oh, to have even raised the idea of a public airing would have been looked upon as sheer insanity, and would no doubt have brought 'the priest and the doctor in their long coats running over the fields'.

A consistent theme running through rural Ireland is the inability of the people to challenge the resolute belief systems of an introspective communal ethos. Many choose to live, suffocate and die in a 'safe', benighted fog. My parents thought that the manifestation might simply go away, given time.

We were halfway through the ordeal when the two boys were moved to the girls' bedroom: Rosaleen and I in one bed, Mark and John in theirs, against the opposite wall. The parents hoped to prove by this experiment that the scourge was confined to one room only. It surely wouldn't have the nerve to travel. The electric light was left burning in the hallway; ever since the beginning of the episode the thought of darkness was unbearable.

So all four of us lay there in the stillness, terrified and longing for the sleep that would transport us from this nightmare into gentle, soothing dreams. I lay with the blankets clutched tight around my face, my eyes concentrating on my brothers as they too tried to sleep, and hoped and prayed that 'it' would stay away.

I kept watch over the boys, snug in their blankets, and willed them *not to move a muscle*. I felt that the merest shift from them would bring on the haunting. The sheer dread of those hours carved such fearful pathways in my psyche that even now the most innocent knock on a door or tap on a table has the power to jangle me.

Was God listening to my prayers that first night? I do not know. For about an hour I watched and waited, and then it happened. What I witnessed next was terrifying.

The strike was sudden, swift and brutal. The boys' mattress lifted clear of the horizontal, hovered for a second or two above the frame and, in one brisk, motion, sent Mark and John crashing to the floor. We all dashed screaming from the room. We set up a howling that was as uncontrollable as it was unreasoning and seemed destined to stretch over an entire lifetime. I felt certain even at that moment that I would never have need to scream like that again. A turning-point had been reached.

We had hardly slept during those first three weeks, and that was bad enough. Now we had to contend with a new and frightening development: the first assault.

My parents decided to take John to the shrine at Knock
— an appropriate place if only because of its name.
They'd pray for a solution that would give him a few
nights' release, and the rest of us some sleep. My mother,
like so many women of her generation, was devoted to
Our Lady and had visited the shrine many times.

The village of Knock, County Mayo, is a famous place
of pilgrimage. On 21 August 1879 the Blessed Virgin
Mary allegedly appeared to 15 locals. This apparition
remained for two hours, and was not witnessed again.
The incident was unusual in that the BVM neither
moved nor delivered a message. At other more famous
sites, such as Lourdes and Fatima, the witnesses have all
received communications.

She appeared on the gable wall of the village church as
the central figure in a tableau, flanked by St John the
Evangelist and St Joseph. To the left of the group was an
altar with a large cross surrounded by adoring angels,
and at its foot a lamb. Not a word was spoken during the
apparition, but many words have been written about it
since.

The pilgrimage undertaken by my parents appeared to
bear fruit. While they prayed with John in Knock, we
waited at home for results; 26 days had passed since the
haunting began.

All seemed well that night. The sleep we yearned for
was restored; the house was quiet, there was a glimmer of
hope in the long darkness. The Virgin Mary had routed
our weird visitor, had sent it packing for good.

Or so we thought. The following day John and my
parents returned, sleepless and distraught. The entity
had followed them all the way to Knock and back; it had
kicked up a racket under the bed in the B&B they stayed
in and continued its pestering in the car. John could not
sit anywhere now: stool, chair, sofa, bed, it followed him

everywhere. It got to the point where sending him to school was a risk that could not be taken.

In the sixth and final week of the 'visitation' a third mass was offered in the room, but to no avail. The racket continued as before. The hands of the most devout — several holy men and women from various orders and parishes — and relics of the most sainted were laid on John's head, but the evil cacophony persisted, wreaking havoc in our hearts and all around us.

We thought things could get no worse, but they did. A presence began to move across the mattress of the haunted bed. We could see the depressions made by what looked like a four-footed animal as it roamed around on the pliant surface. Mother bravely extended her hands to see if she could touch it, only to recoil in horror when she made contact with what appeared to be the motile coat of either a dog or a goat-like creature.

This startling development demanded more urgent measures. All the prayers that had been said, all the masses offered in the room, had come to nothing. Father O'Neill decided he would have to inform the archbishop, who in turn authorised the visit of an exorcist from England. Even as a child I understood the gravity of this development. The exorcist was the last resort and our final hope.

Among Christians, only the Catholic Church offers a formal rite of exorcism, the *Rituale Romanum*, a ceremony which dates from 1614. Less solemn exorcisms are performed by Protestant ministers. To 'exorcise' does not mean to cast out but rather to place the invading spirit 'on oath'; the exorcist invokes the power of God to compel the entity to act in a way contrary to its wishes. The Bible tells us that Jesus cast out many devils, but did not exorcise, because he had no need to call on an authority higher than Himself.

Most exorcisms are performed by a priest or minister, assisted by a junior cleric, a physician and, if need be, a family member.

I can only remember that December morning in monochrome. Me at the parlour window, my chin resting on the sill, staring out at the mist-veiled mountains, the dew-beaded grass, a crow perched still and deathlike on a fence post. All quiet, shrouded, hidden, as if the world held a finger to its lips in a warning hush.

And then suddenly through the mist in the lane, two dark figures advancing on the house: the exorcist and his assistant. Then my mother coming into frame, hurrying to meet them. I see hands gripping hands, an exchange of voiceless greetings. All at once they appear in the kitchen: serious, etiolated men in black soutanes, saying little, patting heads, calling John 'my child'.

We knew the priests were very important men because they wasted no time on smiles or badinage. They refused the proffered tea with the slightest of gestures; such economy of speech and movement hinted at the energy they needed to conserve for the dreadful task that lay before them. They were the divine specialists come to do battle with the ghostly insubstantial.

This was the beginning of the end of our sorrow. There was a palpable feeling in the air that morning; a kind of realisation that these men of God would cleanse the house and release us all at last.

At their request the room had been stripped of its remaining furniture: the wardrobe and the bed. On a small table mother had assembled a crucifix, two candles and a bowl of holy water. The exorcist carried a small black suitcase; the assistant helped him into a surplice and draped a violet satin stole about his shoulders before they entered the room. They shut the door quietly and firmly behind them, at once shutting themselves in and ourselves out. Mother sighed and crossed herself as she turned away from the closed door. For now, it seemed she would not be needed. I could feel the strain of all those tortured weeks begin to ease as she willed those capable and ministering men to deliver us from the danger that threatened.

We children were banished to Helen's home for the remainder of the day, and were at once curious and glad to be absent. The exorcist and his assistant stayed in the locked room for many hours, not emerging until they'd completed their mission.

At the end of it all they drank tea, then went with us to the now-purified room. There we all prayed together; the clergymen assured us that Great-aunt Rose had been finally laid to rest and would never bother us again. With that they were gone. They left as quietly and unobtrusively as they had come.

The blind faith we had in those men was matched by the fearless actions of my mother following their departure. The linoleum was laid down again, the room's furniture was reinstalled and the bed returned to its proper place by the window. We all assembled and said the rosary as we'd done so many times before — except that this time our prayers were of thanksgiving, and were uninterrupted.

Afterwards we remained kneeling in the glorious silence. Mother, in one final act of faith, lifted John in her arms and placed him on the bed. He didn't wail or remonstrate but lay there and waited. (It is perhaps worth mentioning that throughout the weeks of haunting John never showed any degree of fear or panic, nor did he cry or question why this was happening to him.) Prior to this, just sitting on the bed for a few seconds was enough to bring on the knocking. This time there was nothing, just complete and total peace. There was no doubt that the entity had gone, that the spirit of our great-aunt had finally been laid to rest.

That night we all went to bed with relief coupled with a lingering nervousness, not quite believing that we were free of the haunting at long last.

There was, however, a cruel epilogue to the tale. In the early hours we were awakened by our dog Carlo howling in the yard. The doleful cries lasted for about five minutes, fading into a whimpering lament before ceasing. The following morning, to our great dismay, we found Carlo dead. His poor little twisted body lay where he sometimes slept: under the wheelbarrow. We were in no doubt that the departure of our 'visitor' and Carlo's death were linked.

From that day forward, and after six hellish weeks, we were never bothered again. A miracle had been worked and a blessed calm descended, unlacing every knot of fear in our hearts and in every room of the house. All alarm and panic were sucked clean away with the entity's parting, but not surprisingly it left a residue of trauma that was harder to expel. None of us could sleep, eat or study normally for a long time after.

Our mother never told us what kind of ritual had been performed and we never dared to ask; she took that secret knowledge to the grave. As I contemplate it, more than 30 years later, this event still has the power to amaze and unnerve me. Something awesome happened then, a subtle adjusting of perceptions that set me on another path, another journey, a spiritual questing for knowledge and answers that has never abated.

At the young age of eleven, a veil had been drawn back to reveal to me an altogether alien reality. I came to know that the dead did indeed live in a dimension I could not see. This realisation reinforced my belief in God because it was His power that had finally laid old Rose finally to rest. Those two exorcists truly carried divine power into our home that day, in their healing hands and trusting hearts. They asked nothing in return, but every prayer I have said since contains an acknowledgement of the selfless love their act demonstrated to me.

What had visited us all those years ago? It's common knowledge that the word poltergeist derives from the German *poltern*, to knock, and *Geist*, ghost. Our visitor answered most of the criteria attributed to such phenomena: the activity started and stopped suddenly, it lasted for a number of weeks, it always occurred when a particular individual or agent — my brother John — was present, and it was most active during the hours of darkness.

But what reinforces for me the notion that it was indeed the ghost of our great-aunt is the fact that in many cases the spirits of the dead will knock and scratch and move heavy objects. Mischievous and malevolent energies, on the other hand, are characterised by breakages, the throwing of light objects, or physical assault on, or the possession of, the agent.

I cannot accept the theory proposed in the 1930s that poltergeist activity is caused by sexual conflicts generated during the onset of puberty: projections of repressed emotions, such as anger and hostility. The writer Stephen King further enlarged this idea in his novel *Carrie* and in the film of the same name. In King's fiction the teenage Carrie, victim of a repressed upbringing and bullying classmates, finally unleashes all her anger by the power of telekinesis.

Yes, my siblings and I were all either approaching or experiencing puberty; and yes, we were an unhappy bunch of fearful, confused children. Yet it's difficult to believe that a nine-year-old boy could either deliberately or unconsciously cause such upheaval. The theory of 'repression' mooted by psychologists has since been rejected by some eminent researchers in the field, who have gathered enough convincing evidence to drive a coach and horses through the hypothesis.

Dr Martin Israel, a clergyman and senior lecturer in pathology at the University of London, believes that spirits are rarely evil, but are entities confused and trapped within the aura of a living person. (The aura is a subtle emanation that surrounds all living things and provides a host for occult phenomena.) Dr Israel asserts that such entities are family members or friends of the victim, trying to complete their business on the earthly plane.

Given what I know about Great-aunt Rose and the nature of her life, it does not surprise me that she had unfinished business to attend to.

The timing of this visitation is significant also. The spirit showed up on 31 October. For the ancient Celts this day – Hallowe'en, or Samhain – was the most sacred of all their festivals, a solar feast dedicated to the Lord of the Dead. They believed that on the eve of Samhain (*Oíche Shamhna*) the dead arose and roamed abroad, creating mischief by blighting crops and causing chaos in homes up and down the land. The Celts also held that the veil between this world and the next was at its frailest at Samhain, making it easier for dead and living to communicate with one another.

But what I find most interesting about the Celtic mythology is that, during the darkest hours of the night – in our case around 3am – the Lord of the Dead was believed to summon all lost souls in order that their sentences in the hereafter might be reviewed. Often this meant that condemned souls were destined to spend 12 months on the earthly plane in *animal form*.

I have stressed 'animal form' because it's intriguing and very curious how the animal motif figures in all this. There was the goat that drove us to our great-aunt's door; the invisible dog or goat that my mother felt moving on the bed; finding our dog Carlo dead the morning following the exorcism. Bizarre coincidences or evidence of an ancient truth? God alone knows.

Why John? It has been well documented that spirits will attach themselves to the spirit of an innocent child in order to cleanse and purify themselves; in much the same way we attach ourselves to saints, or a favoured relative who has 'passed over', to help us and guide us here on the physical plane. Do we know what we set in train when we pray thus, and what turbulence we create in the ethereal regions with our petitions and requests?

Perhaps Great-aunt Rose knew that by beseeching the youngest and purest mind she would get the response she craved and get it quickly. We prayed as much for John's deliverance as we did for hers. She released him when she'd finally found release herself. It took an enormous amount of effort and prayer to bring this about. Is it too much to assume that refusing to be loving in this life guarantees unrest in the next? And if this is the case then why do so many of us find it so difficult to make the qualities of love and goodness the mainstay of our lives here?

The Master and The Provo

Two months after the exorcism I sat the eleven-plus examination. I did not make the grade; my concentration had suffered as a result of the 'visitor'. The homework, during the period of haunting, rarely got completed and Master Bradley administered the beatings as usual. The burden of not being able to explain to him the real reason for my negligence was yet another injustice to be borne.

At any rate the Master had not encouraged success in the classroom. Lisnamuck primary school inspired neither confidence nor excellence in its pupils. Since we were mostly the progeny of farmers and labourers it was assumed that the collective aspirations of parents and pupils were not very high. This unspoken ethos excused abysmal teaching methods and crushed the hopes of an untold number of bright pupils.

The priest, the doctor and teacher had absolute power in those days. No one challenged their despotic status within the rural community. My parents accepted without question the brutality of the Master. Those frequent episodic sicknesses, sore heads and sore stomachs that excused us from school were viewed as a malingering tactic rather than with the concern they deserved. It never seemed to occur to my elders that such obvious 'unhappiness' must have had far deeper psychological roots. My father had been beaten by his own teacher and he reasoned that what was good enough for him was good enough for his offspring. We stopped looking for his sympathy when we discovered, to our great dismay, that his general response was to give us a further clout for having 'upset the Master' in the first place.

Mother, being a woman, was more disposed to discussion than attack. Never once, however, did she bring the Master to task. He was left to continue his sadistic practices while his innocent pupils bent and buckled under the tyranny.

The torture did finally end – in June 1971 – when I left that awful school and the ire of Master Bradley for good. The scourge had been expunged from my life, but the damage to my psyche would take longer to heal.

However Master Bradley was not the only teacher employed in the ritual abuse of pupils at that time; my Uncle Robert, also a headmaster, was dishing out the same brutality to the innocents of Altyaskey, another parish school in the vicinity of Draperstown.

Robert, my father's older brother, had been the chaperon on my parents' honeymoon and their 'spirited' tour guide to the sites of Dublin. He had also been confidant to Great-aunt Rose and, as such, bursar to the family fortune. Much of his income derived from two establishments of alcoholic refreshment in Draperstown. Both pubs were bequeathed to him by his Uncle Mark – Rose's brother – on his demise. Apart from all this, he owned three farms, even though he would have had difficulty distinguishing a turnip from a sprout.

He had a real talent for attracting money into his bank account, did Robert. He was always in the right place at the right time, somehow contriving to be near a 'profitable' deathbed and guiding a trembling hand in its final scrawl. As the occupant croaked himself into the hereafter Robert would emerge into the light of day, a triumphant smile softening his stern face.

My uncles rarely smiled. It was as if to do so showed weakness. Worse still, it might have indicated a willingness to forget themselves completely and part with some of their precious cash. Money was for hoarding, not for spending or — God forbid — giving away. So they lived their lives:

> Keeping the soul unjostled,
> The pocket unpicked,
> The fancies lurid,
> And the treasure buried.

Robert, though, in his defence, proved to have a wealthy store of knowledge as well as money. He was an avid absorber of literature, had astonishing retentive powers for precise figures and facts and — what impressed me most — he carried around a repository of grammatical knowledge that would have put the most learned linguist to shame. I had reason to mine this seam when during a university course I sought his sagacity in differentiating the properties of the transitive and ditransitive verb. He solved the mystery with a studied casualness that impressed me no end. Oliver Goldsmith would have recognised his sort:

> The village all declar'd how much he knew;
> 'Twas certain he could write, and cipher too:
> Lands he could measure, terms and tides presage,
> And e'en the story ran that he could gauge.

It was clear to me that he possessed a prodigious intellect; yet he chose to live, for purely monetary reasons, an irrational life. Intelligence and common sense did not sit comfortably in his head. As for spirituality, well how could it even get a look in? Oh yes, he went to mass and attended to his duties, so to speak; the actor on that votary stage 'receiving' every Sunday. Sure what would the neighbours say if a man missed mass? A body could not be seen to be lying in his bed on a Sunday of all days, boys a dear.

Indeed earlier in life Robert had actually contemplated the religious life. At 18 he had aspirations for the priesthood and was sent to Maynooth College to realise them. I do not believe this to have been a genuine vocation. Personally I never saw him display those attributes — love, kindness and compassion for one's fellow man — which surely must be uppermost in one who wishes to answer such a calling. However, in those less enlightened days, a family's reputation was greatly enhanced if a son or daughter submitted to the dog-collar or wimple. I am sure lots of bullying was carried out — vocation or not — by those parents eager to acquire that pious sheen of respectability.

After two years Robert left Maynooth, and went to college in London to study English, emerging four years later with a passport into the teaching profession. The reluctant prelate was to become the hesitant schoolmaster.

Yet, for all his achievements, the most enduring image I have of him is of his substantial presence blocking our kitchen doorway. He'd lean against the frame, the thumb of his left hand tucked under a lapel, like an Old Bailey barrister about to deliver a crucial summing up, observing mother as she laboured in the kitchen. She rarely sat down to talk to him. She was always busy — baking, cooking or washing — and the Master seemed to have all the time in the world. In retrospect I think she should have told him to bugger off, but she didn't dare.

He had a perpetual air of unease about him, and I sense this was due to the fact that in 40 years he had not allowed a penny to be spent without regretting it. Unfortunately he carried around the evidence of each of those painful transactions in his long face, his overbearing stance and his eagerness to eschew all those social occasions where he might be required to part with a bob or two: the parish hall jumble sale, the variety concert for political prisoners, mutual congress with a fellow drinker over a pint in the pub.

You could feel the chary diction running through him: 'Give them an inch and they'll be in on top of me, cleaning me out of house and home and land and all my folding money, and then where would a body be atall, atall?'

So the guard was always on duty about his person; he might as well have hung a 'keep out' sign round his neck.

Uncle Robert might have been rich by anyone's standards but his fortune was rarely debited, even for necessary items. He drove cars and wore clothes until they literally fell apart. He had a 'funeral' suit and a suit for everyday wear. Over each he'd put on a grey raincoat, buttoned to the neck even on the hottest day. Though this layer of plastic acted as protection from the elements, I suspect that its primary function was to conceal a rather cavalier attitude towards personal hygiene.

Following the passing of his Aunt Rose, Robert moved from the house he shared with his brothers James and Edward into the cottage he'd inherited from her. Edward joined him there soon after, having discovered that he couldn't live in amity with the fussy James. James, for his part, was more than happy to be rid of both brothers; now he could lay sole claim to the bleak dwelling that was the parental home.

My uncles were like feral cats in the face of their diminishing kin, coveting all they could from the recent dead to the detriment of a weaker sibling. They all lived and languished and died in the place of their birth, fearing that to stray into the wider world to live constructive, fulfilling lives would mean a smaller share of the spoils in the end. So they chose to stay stuck, frozen in a permanent winter, waiting to move in for the kill, no matter how long it took, willing another to die first and blaming everyone but themselves for the fatuous choices they had made.

I have never understood this. Surely life should be about changing and progressing and righting the wrongs of past generations, rather than repeating their transgressions. However, lessons are not so easily learned when one chooses to remain blind to the needs of others.

After he retired from teaching — and making life thoroughly miserable for the pupils of Altyaskey primary school — Robert continued an existence of structured monotony. Each morning he would drive his blue Ford Anglia at a steady pace to Draperstown, his white hands clutching the steering wheel in a firm ten-to-two grip, the eyes steady on the road ahead. He took his vehicle and his life seriously, not wanting to lose either prematurely. He had too much money to look after, and this responsibility had nurtured a keen sense of self-preservation.

It became an obsession with him. He admitted to mother once that, before using a pedestrian crossing in Belfast, he preferred to wait until a good crowd had gathered; then he'd 'get well into the middle of them' before crossing. He reckoned that if you happened to be on the margins you ran the chance of being clipped and tossed by a reckless motorist. And then where would a man be atall, atall?

On rare occasions mother would send me with Robert to Draperstown to buy some item she'd forgotten or was low on, such as tea or sugar. You might wonder why the Master couldn't have run the errand himself. It never seemed to occur to him to offer, and mother was probably too timid to ask.

I hated those tense, silent journeys. He had the annoying habit of halting before corners and sounding the horn several times before moving on. Once, I had the temerity to ask him why, and he took his hands from the wheel.

'See, if I didn't do that,' he said in all earnest, 'a young gype could be round that corner like the divil, and could be into us like *that*.' He stressed the last word with a loud clap of the raised hands.

There were many corners between Robert's house and Draperstown so the jaunt was a lengthy one. You could have walked there and back faster.

Sadly that Anglia would never realise its dashing potential under Robert's guidance. On finally reaching the town he'd crawl onto High Street and devote all his energy to the formidable act of parallel parking. This was a complicated business involving much mirror work and signals, the head roving from side to side, gauging distances and checking for those ubiquitous 'young boys' who were all, he'd convinced himself, out to do him damage. The steering wheel would be twisted and fed through his powerful hands, and all the while the rustling raincoat swished and swore in protest.

Robert's own grocery list reflected the lacklustre menu he and Edward enjoyed every day: bread and butter, bacon and eggs, sausages, potatoes and milk. He marched from greengrocer to butcher to baker, conducting the transactions over exchanges of gossip concerning the weather, politics, and who had died – or was about to. Being the schoolmaster he was accorded the same respect as the doctor and the priest; this daily intercourse with the town's shopkeepers was the pivot on which his whole day turned.

He'd buy the *Irish News* last and, after he'd stowed the provisions in the boot of the car, would sit and scan the obituaries column for news of God's most recent withdrawals from life's great piggy bank. All the adults around me – my parents included – took a morbid interest in death. This had little to do with the contemplation of their own mortality, because if it had then they would surely have led more productive and happy lives, packing in as much as possible before the final curtain. To paraphrase Dr M Scott Peck: In order to learn how to live, we have to come to terms with our own death, because our death reminds us of the limit of our existence. Only when we become aware of the brevity of our time can we make full use of that time.

When Robert scanned the deaths column, Dr Peck's reasoning did not figure. He was hoping to discover a name he knew. His joy lay in being the first to impart the 'bad news' to mother or the neighbours and observe their shock. There was satisfaction to be had in relaying the sad tidings just so long as they didn't affect the bearer. Such are the compensations of an empty life.

That newspaper was not only fodder for his morbid curiosity but had an astonishing assortment of other functions. Yellowing copies were employed as seat covers in the car. More pages protected the table at meal times, and he used others to light the fire, and dry the dishes. I don't doubt that it also did duty as toilet roll in the outside privy, although I cannot confirm this, having neither need nor inclination to visit it.

He'd usually stop by our house on his way home from town and take up position in the kitchen doorway, obstructing our passage from house to yard. If we children were indoors when he arrived then we were virtually under house arrest, and if we happened to be in the yard then we'd have to prolong our play until he left. Either way we were too afraid to squeeze past him.

He'd give mother the lowdown on the latest gossip. He carried with him an encyclopaedic knowledge of every family in the parish, seemingly stretching back to St Matthew's book of generation, when Judas begat Phares and Zara of Thamar; and Phares begat Esrom; and Esrom begat Aram. ...

Robert was in his element if he had a death to announce. He'd stand there, my captive mother nodding and sighing, while he rattled out a tracery of the deceased's ancestral connections with all the skill of a master genealogist. He'd pick up tributaries of names and details, and join them to the main family flux with facts and dates, while mother listened patiently. She had somehow to simultaneously keep track of the rising scones and those convoluted histories without causing offence.

'His mother would have been a Martha McAtamney from outside Ballymuck,' Robert would intone, 'who got married on a son of the Buffer McVeighs — or were they the Butcher McVeighs? Anyway they owned a couple of farms out by the lough shore until one of the Mickey McSquirtys married into them in nineteen and fifty-two and that was the end of it all.'

He would pause for breath and emphasis, and to test mother's attentiveness. If there was one thing Robert disliked it was inattentiveness in his audience. Too many years spent in front of oscitant pupils had made him uncompromising. Mother had learned this lesson too and was ever alert.

'Is that so?' she'd say. 'I thought the McSquirty girls were fine lassies.'

'Not a bit of it! Didn't the Lily wan turn the young boy's head completely, put him to the bad altogether, lost the head and the two farms and the pair of them drunk it out. Aye, a bad pack. It was in the breed of them that wee weakness was there. Then another of them married a Dan McFadden. Dy'mine him? I say he was a Dan McFadden!'

The voice would have risen to a whine because mother had turned, perhaps to rescue a scone in the nick of time. But in a second she'd be back, feigning interest yet again with a placatory comment.

'You don't say, Robert. Is that so?'

'Aye, them McFadden crowd weren't up to much either.'

The litany would continue. Each sentence marching out to the beat of an invisible drum.

'He was a son of a cousin of an uncle of Stuttering Paddy's. Y'mine him, a low set, stout boy with a squint, dragged the leg a bit, nivver out of the pub either. Used to see him spraghalling up Mary Pat's back, stotious.' (By which he meant that he'd often observed the character in question staggering into Mary Pat's public house by the rear entrance.) 'Couldn't get enough of that drigging. His mother would have been a half-sister of Jamie the Snout's. She would have been a Thompson to her maiden name.'

'Thompson, that sounds like a Protestant name, doesn't it?' mother would say with sudden attentiveness.

'Aye, it is, but the oul' boy was a turncoat, back in nineteen and forty-seven. He had an illegitimate wain to a daughter of Johnny the Slap's, a wee fat lady, wasn't too right in the head. A kind of a clatt of a blade from up the country or y'know deed begod it could have been down the country, can't mine right, put him astray altogether. The priest had to be called and didn't they fine him dead in a sheugh outside Ballygosidewards at half five in the morning on the fifteenth of June nineteen and thirty-six, stiff with drink more than anything else.'

'Is that so Robert? God, that drink's a terrible curse.'

'Aye. Sure they say when a man gets a feed of that poison he doesn't know whether he's living or dead. Tarra stuff. ... A bad crowd, aye. And that was the end of that.'

There would follow an uneasy silence while mother ingested all this information and Robert raised his cap, to scratch his crown with the middle finger. He'd replace it an inch or two more towards the back of his head with an air of satisfaction, pleased to have had his say so heatedly and eloquently.

'Aye, that's the way the oul' thing goes,' he'd remark while studying a patch of ceiling.

My mother, eager for closure and fearful he might start up again, would offer something like: 'God, I can't believe that Wee Jamie's gone. He was a harmless cretur.'

'Aye, that's the way it goes,' Robert would add after a long pause. 'Comes to us all, boys a dear. S'pose a body would need tae go tae a wake and funeral — on account of Big Frenkie. And that means a mass card havin' to be bought. Pity a body couldn't buy a wheen of them in bulk; you'd save a quare bit, so you would.'

There was the phantom Frenkie again; his name seemed always to emerge when someone had expired. Either he was a very gregarious man or had spread his seed far in the course of an ill-spent youth.

On one occasion, however, Robert got things confused. He announced to mother that a mutual acquaintance of theirs — one Lizzy McCrudden or 'Lizzy the Dizzier' — had died. In a state of shock she sped posthaste to Draperstown to buy the obligatory mass card. Imagine her astonishment when on the return journey she met Lizzy pedalling her bike into town. There had obviously been two Lizzy McCruddens in the locality — either that or Robert, disgusted at the slow death-rate in the parish and having no shocking news to report, had made it up by way of compensation.

Yet fate was to get its own back on Robert. He himself made the pages of the *Irish News*, though not the obituaries column. One bright August morning, while he trundled along 'twixt Draperstown and his homestead, rations in the boot and eyes steady on the road, Robert's car was hijacked.

As the Anglia mounted the first hill out of town, a man toting a gun jumped from behind a hedge and ordered Robert to stop. He'd been hijacked by a member of the Provisional IRA. The Provo took possession of the car and sped off, leaving the Master dazed and stranded in the middle of the road, his arms raised in an attitude of surrender.

Mother was out at the clothes-line at the time, awaiting Robert's regular visit. She was astonished to see the Anglia flying past the gate, doing, she estimated, a very respectable, rip-roaring 90mph.

The car was found two days later with everything intact, save the groceries; the gunman had obviously been hungry. Robert dined out on this story with tremendous frequency in the days that followed, re-enacting the drama for the butcher, the baker, the candlestick-maker and whoever else would listen.

He'd play the twin roles in the drama: himself and the Provo. My mother and I heard it more often than we cared to.

'He jumped out of that hedge like a fox,' Robert would tell us yet again. '"Get out quick, out quick, out quick," says he. Begod, y'know I think he said it five times. Aye, as if a man needed to be told five times, wi' a gun pointin' at his head.'

'God, what did you do atall?' mother would enquire yet again.

'Well, what could a body do but put me hands up in the air? And I put them up good and high too, and y'know, God, he was in the car and away like a whitred before I knew it, the rips and roars of him, you'd a heard him in Cork, begod. That wee car'll niver be the same again, so it won't.'

'To hell with the oul' car, Robert, isn't your life more important than an oul' tekelin?' my mother would say, voicing my own thoughts.

'Aye well, I suppose,' he'd venture, not at all convinced.

'Well, did you get a good look at him?'

'Aw aye. A young hairy bugger, down the back and round the face and everywhere you looked. Should have been in a zoo, aye locked up. A zoo would have been the best place for that boy. God, it's a wile thing when a man can't conduct a wee bitta business without havin' to come through the like a that. What's the country comin' to anyway, anyway, anyway? The whole place's gone to hell completely.'

He'd then wait for the praise and sympathy he felt was his by right. Mother wouldn't disappoint him.

'God, Robert you're a tight one. I would of died on the spot, so I would, as true as God.'

For weeks afterwards Robert was the hero, and the humble Anglia had at last experienced the passion and fury of life in the fast lane — something Robert would never know.

Life in Northern Ireland has changed a great deal since that incident. So much so that it's alleged that the same hirsute, gun-toting Republican became a member of our recently formed Legislative Assembly up at Stormont, pronouncing with gravitas on the morals of the nation. I can feel Robert beginning to rotate in his grave as I write these lines.

Occasionally the Master had other reasons for waylaying mother. He needed her help when dealing with his problem brother Edward. Edward had a liking for an alcoholic beverage or two — which was not at all surprising given that he had to share living quarters with Robert, which cannot have been easy. The Master rarely touched a drop himself. Edward's relationship with the booze was therefore sporadic and for that reason all the more intense when he got the chance. Robert could not 'be doing with this atall, atall'. He spent a great deal of his time pronouncing on the morality of others, after all, and could ill afford the taint of Edward's profligacy.

It is a pity that the austere and abstemious Robert never allowed himself the pleasures of drink or courtship. Frivolity was a stranger to him. I feel sad that Robert, with all his money, knowledge and that dry sense of humour he had, did not permit himself the joy of sharing it. He might have had a different life entirely. In fact I'm sure of it.

You could easily tell when he'd come to discuss the misdeeds of the errant Edward rather than a death or the weather. He'd adopt a brooding stance in the doorway, his florid face and uneasy manner signalling a deviation from his fixed routine. My mother, reading him accurately, would ask what was wrong, and he'd simply respond with: 'It's him.'

It was an idiosyncrasy of father and Robert that they'd never use the other's first name. The personal pronoun was employed instead, which often led to some confusion. So mother would have to lob a guess.

'Who? James?'

And Robert would glare at her.

'Naw, *him*!' he'd retort. 'That other boy.'

Since there were just the two of them it could only be Edward, so after an 'Oh, Edward' from mother, he'd move on.

'I don't know what's to be done with him, anyway, anyway, anyway.' Another mannerism was to put stress on the last word in a sentence and repeat it several times when voicing annoyance.

'Went out the morning there to find him splayed out on the hay,' Robert would continue. 'Bottle of Powers up to the head, gluggin' away like a dosser. What's to be done atall, atall, atall?'

With the outburst over, mother would take control, and ring the doctor. Dr O'Connor would then prepare the necessary paperwork for Edward's swift admission to the substance-abuse clinic in Derry. Later in the day the guilty Edward would appear at our house looking tired, emotional and — dare I say it — happy. Robert, accompanied by father, would convey him in the Anglia to 'detox hell'.

Robert visited us by day; Edward would invariably show up in the early evening; we'd be part of his ceilidhing routine at the homes in the neighbourhood. He liked it best when my father was not around. He could drop his guard then and be himself.

Edward always seemed to me to be the most approachable, and the sanest, of the brood. A positive side effect of his desire for the drink was that it rendered him more genial than his brothers. He had spirit in more ways than one.

He worked and passed his leisure hours in bibbed overalls and a checked shirt whose collar points were permanently curled under the pressure of his chin. In Ballinascreen and the surrounding locality the customary headgear of the farming man was a cloth cap. It was a multipurpose item: it kept the hair in place, covered baldness and a slipshod grooming routine.

I saw Edward's world as stretching no farther than home and farm. He plunthered and pedalled the lanes and roads, living within these narrow perimeters. He experienced the spring showers, the summer heat, the falling leaves and snow and was unaware that these shifts of the seasons were the only change he'd be likely to experience.

When given the tea he'd talk and slurp, pausing only to take alligator bites of the bread. It seemed that he'd have barely started before the cap would be shoved back onto his head. He'd lean back on the chair and belch loud his appreciation.

There were times when he'd lighten the monotony of his life with music. Particularly when laid low with the booze — and with our parents out of sight — he'd pitch high on the harmonica, squeezing out notes that surged into melodies we children could identify. That mouth organ brought forth his cringing inner self, a beauty that had never been allowed to breathe. Sometimes we'd spoil it all by joining in with paper combs, all of us sounding like a swarm of bees in a jam jar.

On hearing the latch lift and our parents' footsteps in the hallway Edward would swiftly stow the instrument in the bib of his overalls, we'd discard our combs and reluctantly return to the heavy, gloomy atmosphere that preceded father like a thundercloud. With that, Edward would be gone, the ceilidh over.

And at one stage Master Robert, envying Edward's musical skill and never one to be outdone, bought himself a fiddle. In the evenings he'd fill the doorway and our kitchen with a blare of rasping discordancies. He'd stand there, the elbow sawing wildly, the raincoat going crazy with such alien exertion, and so inveigle my hapless mother into a 'Name That Tune' contest she could never win.

After each frenzied movement Robert would stop and ask, 'Now ye know what that'un was, don't ye?' And mother would try vainly with: '*The Mountains of Mourne*?'

'Not atall,' Robert would remonstrate heavily. 'Boys-oh, how could that be *The Mountains of Mourne*? What kind of ears have ye on ye atall, atall? It's *Are Ye Right There Michael, Are Ye Right*? Here, listen again.'

And off he'd go with another torturous rendering. When Robert finally left, mother would heave a great sigh of relief and say: 'God I hate tae see him comin' with that bloody fiddle. Sounds like he's scraping an ashplant over the arse of a bucket, so it does. Has he no sense?'

But Robert could neither accept defeat nor take a hint, no matter how many scoreless results mother had chalked up. He persisted until finally all the strings broke, much to his annoyance and her delight.

Leaving the Sunlight for the Gloom

Arthur, the oldest McKenna brother, I never got to know; he died before I was old enough to form an opinion of him, but my memory is of a remote figure, tall and stern, the nose a bumpy outcrop on a craggy face. He wore a felt hat like father's and a long, belted gaberdine which made him look very sinister and unapproachable. I saw him once in a far field, shaking a stick and roaring at a cow, which didn't augur well.

On Arthur's demise James became the guardian of the family home: a brooding, two-storey dwelling about a mile from our house. This was where my father and his siblings had been born. It was a strange, silent place with a disquieting air about it as if some baleful event had caused everything to atrophy long, long ago.

The house never seemed occupied somehow. On approaching it you got the feeling that at some point in the dim past its dwellers, moved by some supernatural calling, had suddenly got up and wandered off into the fields, never to be seen again.

But as you drew nearer you found that someone, against his better judgement, had decided not to heed that call from the other world, and was therefore doomed to languish in the house, regretful of that decision. That person was Uncle James.

The back door was always agape yet the clucking hens in the yard were the only signs of life. Those sinister lines in *Flannan Isle* come to mind.

We stood a moment, still tongue-tied:
And each with black foreboding eyed
The door, ere we should fling it wide,
To leave the sunlight for the gloom.

His yard bore the unvarying features of all the homesteads I knew. The machinery of agribusiness stood about like pieces of sculpture in an outdoor museum. Here: a tractor with the unhitched vertical of a trailer at its rear. There: a defeated hayshaker, blistering and rusting under the hot sun; and a proud baler, forged and new, which obviously did not belong.

The yard was bounded by white-distempered barns, with doors of faded green opening into odd degrees of darkness. As a child I dared not venture beyond those openings for fear of a door slamming shut behind me and locking me in for ever.

Often when we went for a walk on Sunday evenings mother and I would make a social call, but James, forever the misanthrope, didn't see it that way. On hearing our approach he'd appear on the stone step, filthy tea towel in hand, and enquire with a suspicious eye what it was we were 'down about'. No 'Hello, how are you?' here. Friendliness would have meant he approved of us, and that would never do.

Like his brother Arthur, James was tall and grim, hair sticking out from under his cap like ticking from a burst sofa, left eye bigger than the right as if a phantom monocle was permanently wedged in the socket. He wore the regulation uniform of the farmer: laced up boots, plaid shirt, serge trousers with a pair of braces hoisting them high off ankles and paunch, the whole ensemble creased and defeated looking. Most of this apparel would have been bought from an army surplus stall, at a knockdown price, on a fair-day in nearby Maghera.

Precious cash was never wasted on necessities like clothing.

Only when he'd assured himself that his money was safe and that we hadn't come to borrow his precious Morris Minor would we be admitted inside James's lonely homestead. He spent most of his time in the kitchen. I remember every detail of it; the features of that kitchen have stayed in my head like a lacklustre woodcut.

It appeared as though my uncle was more a caretaker than a dweller. No effort had been made to make the place homely. The atmosphere was stale, lacking warmth or welcome. In the kitchen a fire roared and a clock ticked. Even back then I could see the potential that would lie for ever unrealised. The flagged floor and blazing hearth had a brashness about them which didn't quite belong — all that shameless shine and vigour which spoke of merriment and laughter and tankards raised in toast. The floor, polished with the feet of spiritless generations, wanted to be danced upon and explored in all its fullness. And the hearth wanted to warm a whole host of flickering otherness. I could see a Breughel gathering taking shape: wenches in straining bodices, cavorting with their skirts held high; thigh-slapping young bucks in velvet and brocade, making risqué gestures in the shadows. The air craved lively music to cut across the silence and the solitary lamp high up on the raftered ceiling begged for the chance to strike it all to life.

I fear that that kitchen never knew joy of any kind. The floor had to make do with nothing more lively than James's weary tread.

There was a fireplace with a crane crook holding a kettle of water for the tea. At noon the kettle was substituted for a pot of potatoes for the midday meal.

The kitchen had the typical inventory of tired furniture: a brown studded couch, a scrubbed table by the window, two plain wooden chairs dating from the previous century, one of them serving as a rail for a grubby handtowel. As a point of dismal interest there was a glass case, slobbered with innumerable layers of brown gloss paint, which held a display of jaded, willow-patterned Delftware.

On a shelf above the hearth, lined up in order of preference, sat a selection of foodstuffs, all within easy reach. There was a bag of Tate & Lyle sugar, its furled mouth attracting a host of greedy flies. Beside it, a black-and-maroon tea caddy, a pot of Robertson's marmalade and there, towering above all, a drum of Saxa salt, its red-and-yellow label lending some colour to the drabness. From the ceiling hung a strip of yellow, plastic flypaper, the corpses of long-dead insects studding it like so many currants.

The farmhouse had undergone very little change since James's birth. Every time mother and I visited we were met by the same scene, everything preserved and fixed in time, emblems of decades past. It seemed that he was destined to move among these mute observers for ever. Like the furniture, he never changed and was therefore doomed always to live his life in retrospect.

Frequently when we'd call it was to find him engaged in either making tea or cooking a meal, which could only mean one of two things: our timing was always poor or James filled his hours by filling himself. Greed for money usually betokens greed in other areas too. And my uncle was undoubtedly self-centred; no matter how many times we called we were never offered tea or even a chair.

Quite naturally he hated to be disturbed, particularly during the cooking process. On one particular evening we arrived at the 'wrong' time, and happened upon an unforgettable spectacle.

As I recall, the frying pan figured large in his farmhouse cuisine. We stood in the kitchen, inhaling the stench of last week's lard being refried yet again, saw blue smoke surging madly out through the pantry door — as if from the site of a mining disaster. We heard the frantic spluttering of sausages, eggs, bacon and a wee soda farl or two. Then through the furious haze, summoned by mother's call, James emerged, the face roasted off him, his big eye watering fiercely, brandishing the egg-turner like a samurai sword and looking for all the world like an extra from that magnificent 1953 sci-fi B-lister, *It Came From Outer Space*. I need hardly add that he was not especially pleased to see us.

His manner and talk were as cyclical as the seasons. Like his brothers, he lived by a set of obdurate rules, never daring to try anything new lest he discover something different about himself or the world.

He was uncomfortable around people, especially women and children. Our Sunday visits ruffled him slightly; we broke his routine and injected panic in him. He could not settle until the purpose of our call had been established; on learning that it was purely social he'd feel more reassured and begin to talk.

His speech was always hesitant. I never knew if this was a physical impediment or simply the result of indecisive thought. Having spent so long in the same environment he'd begun to resemble the machinery and the hens in the farmyard. His conversations were far from coherent and he had the habit of going off on a wild tangent without warning when he heard something he didn't like.

'That's the weather now,' was his usual conversation opener. 'Maybe a man'll get a bit of hay cut.'

'Sure you could have had that hay cut last week,' my mother would say; she never missed an opportunity to upbraid James for his laziness. 'I don't know what you and Edward are footering about. Before you know it the rain'll be down and then where will ye be?'

James, not wanting to hear the truth about himself, would rummage frantically in his head for something of a less incendiary nature and swiftly change the subject.

'Paddy the Slooter is out of the hospital, I see,' he'd say. 'Maybe there wasn't a wile lot wrong wi' him to start with. People that's goin' nowadays can't thole a thing.' And he'd slurp and snort from the mug of tea and await mother's response.

'What are you sayin'?' She was off again. 'Sure didn't the man have a heart attack? Near died if it hadn't been for wee Mary Lizzie Biddy being there at the time. Bee t' be a wile shock for the wee cretur.'

'She's another one.' James would be getting into his stride now. As with his brothers, women and children did not count for much. 'Has the man broke. A different rig-out on her every Sunday. The man couldn't keep fut till all that and wh ... wa ... wh ... at ... what a ... does she need all them pallions on her for?'

'What are you talkin' about pallions for? What have pallions to do with Paddy's heart?' Mother knew that sympathy was not James's strong suit.

James, seeing he couldn't win, would change the subject yet again, the words queuing up in him to stumble out in a panic. He'd consider the fire in the hearth.

'See-the-price-of-coal-goin'-up-again. Soon be a man'll not be able to live atall, atall. And the butter too wh ... a ... wh ... who's at the back a that a wondir?'

'Sure what are ye buyin' butter for when you could make your own? Have ye no sense? A good churn sittin' out there in the scullery belongin' to your auntie Martha Mary Micky, niver used. God, James, you're a quare one.'

James, sensing defeat, would struggle frantically for a defence.

'Sure isn't the h ... ha ... ha ... han ... hannel on it broke and wh ... a ... wh ... who's gonna fix it anyway, anyway, anyway?'

He clucked and stammered over those challenging 'wh' sounds, and rocked on the chair and flapped his elbows like wings as he spoke. Sometimes, in order to control all his inner commotion, he'd grasp his elbows resolutely in cupped hands, folded forearms now a shield worn high across his chest. But still the machinery of him shook and he'd shift uncomfortably as mother kept the accusations coming.

'Aye, handle broke, me arse! Couldn't ye fix it yourself? Any gulpen with half a brain could fix a bit of a churn. I'm tellin' ye, James, if you had a houseful of wains to feed ye wouldn't be buyin' butter.'

'Aye and what would I be doin' with a clatter of youngsters round me? ... ' And he'd fix me with his large eye, a laser beam of indictment.

'Christ, what sort of craic's that? S'pose ye think ye came into the world with that cap and braces and all on ye.' And so it would go.

James hated to see my mother in his yard. She flung rebuke before him like handfuls of chicken-feed. He was slow. He was lazy. He was everything she was not. No, time never rushed for Uncle James; it sauntered up to him, sidled about a bit and then stood still. He never put off until tomorrow what he could do in six months' time, or better still forget about completely. In short he was procrastination in all its genuflecting glory made flesh.

He was like an old tractor, endlessly stopping and starting up again, with all that moving and jigging about, just itching to roar away. But unlike a tractor James did not have the fuel or power to get himself going. He was destined to stay stuck, spluttering and stalling on the one spot all his life.

Sometimes, as mother and I endured James's disjointed dialogue, a daring hen would wander in and halt in the middle of the floor. It would fix us with an astonished eye, one tentative foot raised high. Such an intrusion wasn't surprising since the door between yard and kitchen stood open for most of the day, and a confused hen would take the stone floor to be the natural extension of its territory.

James would rouse himself from the creaking chair and send the creature flying with a surging of plumage and the skittering skid of talons on stone.

'Get out arrgh that!' he'd bellow. 'Don't know what's to be done with them hens, anyway, anyway, anyway.' It did not seem to occur to him to keep the door shut.

Often in summer the front door was left open too. While he and mother fenced with words, I sometimes wandered down there out of curiosity and boredom. Here the flagged floor gathered itself and made a spotless run down the dim hallway. One thing that can be said in James's defence is that he kept his house relatively clean and tidy.

This corridor was featureless, no pictures or shelves of bric-à-brac to divert me, just a menacing flight of stairs painted in the ugly brown of the glass case. And, snaking up the middle of them, a balding strip of carpet in the colours of dead leaves.

If that ascent into the darkness seems familiar now it's because of a famous movie scene: Norman Bates in Alfred Hitchcock's film *Psycho* climbed the same flight many times to converse with his spectral mother. That staircase was scary even before I'd seen the film. I would stand at the bottom wondering what was up there, and test my courage with a foot on the first tread and a clammy hand on the banister. But the challenge was too much for me; I'd simply retreat into the safety of the hall and view the first floor from afar. Those upper rooms were not for looking into; for me they were the places where the dead roamed; there was a clamour of ghosts up there, I was sure. I imagined the unmade beds and the airless whiff of stale linen; the furniture claw-footed and heavy, and curtains drawn resolutely against the light. There'd be no points of interest to detain the eye, except for one pockmarked mirror, high up on a dun wall, reflecting the listless whole.

The stagnant past of those ancestors came back to haunt me too. In my mind's eye I saw a mother on the base bed in the final throes of giving birth; a raging father shaking an ashplant at the moon as the uncles and aunts, sullen and speechless, stood around among the mayhem.

The thought of old Rose made me back away. I wondered if she'd tried tapping out any messages to her nephews before visiting us. Perhaps she had, but had given up, on realising that nothing would be done for her. Yes, there *were* ghosts up there I was sure, still unaware that their calls would never be answered.

I suppose I naively thought that in every two-storey house, at the top of every flight of stairs, I'd find a bedroom as intriguing as Helen's. I somehow knew even then that I wouldn't find it here. There was no woman to cause scenes of glamorous tumult in that house: no trails of gaudy finery, no clouds of heady scent. Uncle James had neither the curiosity nor generosity to be a lover or husband, so there would never be stiletto heels on those stairs and no peals of breezy laughter to riffle the mildewed air. Festivities were always inappropriate and would never be countenanced; it was a place where the dead lived and the living had — without realising it — already died.

Like his brothers Robert and Edward, James was caged within the flat routines of the fearful and the aimless: those daily jaunts to the village to buy comestibles, the changeless appointment with the confessional of a Saturday evening, the Sunday mass — all duties carried out with the alertness of an automaton and the sincerity of a jester; all to keep the neighbours from talking and the probing clergy from his door.

He ate the same artery-clogging food every day, moved between house and yard, performing his mindless chores; tending to himself in the kitchen, tending to the animals in the yard.

He was prudent in his consumption of alcohol — for purely economic considerations, the cost of the vice being the sobering deterrent. On a Saturday evening, after the trials of the confessional, he'd down a couple of 'half-uns' and a pint of Guinness — no more, no less. This was the only gulp of joy in his grim week.

I ask myself if he ever had dreams to dream or passions to chase or a cause to fight for. Being human I suppose he must have had, perhaps as a young man, but what had happened to blunt the desire to pursue them? What awful hold-up did he perceive on the road out of childhood that made him baulk, and turn back towards the land and that awful house with the promise of hoarded cash in a far-distant future? What a mind-numbing choice to have made, to live in the hopeless past, running the same grainy footage in his head, with all ambitions of love and energy and joyfulness edited out.

My mother would say that 'they didn't take it off the water', which I think implies that such lack of drive was in the genes. I tend to disagree; to me this amounts to a get-out clause for staying stuck in a rut. We all have it within our power to forge our own destinies, blaze our own trails, throw off the yoke of the inherited past and create ourselves anew.

James and his brothers blindly followed in the footsteps of their father who, from all accounts, was an awkward and inward-looking man. It never seemed to occur to the brothers that *they* had the power to change their destinies and live in a more life-enhancing and fulfilling way. They could have learned from the past rather than repeating the same, negative pattern.

I'm reminded of a true story I once heard concerning two brothers. Their father was everything a man should never be: a murderer, a rapist and a drunk. When growing up, the sons absorbed all this negativity, but eventually went their separate ways. In their mid-twenties they were found in different places doing very different things: one had become the CEO of a thriving company, the other a criminal, just like his father. Both were asked the same question: 'How did you turn out to be this way?' Both gave the same answer: 'With a father like that what else could I do?'

Unhappy marriages produce unhappy children, but when we become adults we do have a choice. We can continue being miserable, for the rest of our lives, blaming our parents and believing we are powerless to change. Or we can look around for more affirmative ways to live — and decide to be happy.

This my uncles could so easily have done.

The Big School

In September 1971 I started secondary school in Draperstown. The village takes its name from the Drapers Company of London. During the Plantation of 1610-25, James I of England and VI of Scotland became concerned that not enough British Protestants were taking part in this great colonising enterprise. The quota of applications for the free land – 'free' in the sense of gratis – of Ulster was not being met. James, in exchange for a much-needed injection of investment, granted the London companies, or guilds, the area of land called County Derry, which then became known as Londonderry.

Great importance is placed on names in Northern Ireland. You can quickly deduce a person's religion by the name they give Ulster's second-largest city. The Unionists will stick doggedly to Derry's London- prefix while the Taigs ignore it religiously.

This area of County Derry – see what I mean? – was divided into 12 equal portions and allocated to 12 London companies: mercers, grocers, fishmongers, goldsmiths, skinners, merchant tailors, haberdashers, salters, ironmongers, vintners, clothworkers and drapers. Thus did Draperstown acquire its name.

It's a pretty town, built around a triangular marketplace fringed with lime trees and boasting, like most Irish towns, a church with an impressive spire. In short, one would never suspect that during the late

1800s this sleepy little community, nestling in the shadow of the Sperrin Mountains, could have given birth to a vice that would in time consume the entire country and be roundly denounced from every pulpit up and down the land. Strange though it may seem, it was the Catholic Church which gave rise to the vice in the first place.

In the 1840s Father Theobold Matthew, a fire-and-brimstone cleric and by all accounts a real ray of sunshine, led a total-abstinence crusade throughout England, Scotland and Ireland. It was one of the most successful of its kind and thousands lined up to take the pledge. Among them was an alcoholic physician named Kelly, who had his practice in Draperstown. Uncomfortable with the notion of having to forgo his pleasure, but not wishing to break the pledge, Kelly sought a substitute for the demon drink.

He came up with ether. He had prescribed it by mouth on occasion and knew of its stronger effects. Following a few experiments of his own he shared the knowledge with his friends and a select group of patients who had also taken the pledge. As a result, ether sniffing became rife in Draperstown.

Some years later the government imposed a heavy tax on alcoholic beverages and the police clamped down on home-distilled whiskey. Things looked bleak for the topers of Draperstown — until somebody recalled Kelly's discovery, and decided to exploit it to the hilt. Ether, which was not subject to taxation, was distilled in London and shipped to Draperstown and other places in Ulster by the barrel. The intoxicant proved to be a godsend — especially among the labouring classes — because it was less expensive than whiskey. Moreover, drunkenness could not only be achieved quickly and cheaply several times a day but it was found that ether produced no hangover whatsoever. Perhaps the greatest advantage of all was that if a man or woman was arrested while drunk and disorderly then they were more than likely to be sober by the time the police station was reached.

An English surgeon visiting Draperstown in 1878 was astonished to discover that the main street smelled like the inside of his surgery, where ether was used as an anaesthetic.

I was not aware however of this humble town's colourful past when I was sentenced to five years in its secondary school. In primary school I'd had my self-esteem beaten out of me. In secondary it was my individuality that would suffer.

St Colm's High boasted more teachers, more pupils and more space than Lisnamuck PS. It was a large, bright building with endless corridors and flights of stairs. In keeping with the Catholic ethos it was named after a saint. St Colm's picture hung in the foyer and we prayed to the good man each morning to help us through the day.

I studied nine subjects. There were the essential English and maths. Next came history and geography, which I had no great interest in, since my primary-school experience had failed to arouse in me any curiosity about the world's past, or what it might be made of. There was the pervasive RE of course, and three other subjects that caused me to have nightmares: cookery, Latin and PE.

I wore a grey and turquoise uniform, was given a numbered peg and locker and had to wear slippers while in the school building, to protect the floors. Thus packaged, I became the poet's 'cog in a machine, a thing with one face'.

We switched lessons at the sound of a shrill bell and had to walk in file on the left side of corridors and stairs, to prevent collisions. After a year my inculcation was complete; we moved and talked, shut up and jumped to the peal of shouts or the sting of slaps. School life, to my chagrin, continued to be cruel. There were quite a number of Master Bradley clones — mostly men — who sent waves of fear through me, and a number of lenient, patient women like Miss McKeague, who helped to make life bearable.

The school's then headmaster, Mr Gunn, was a robust gentleman who wore a grey suit and took a keen interest in our personal hygiene. He had need to: we were by and large a dirty, lumpen lot. Each morning after prayers he'd stand on the podium in the assembly hall and obdure us to 'hop into a rubber basin' when we got home and give ourselves a good rub down with soap and water. This instruction was clearly ignored of course as everyone stood about yawning and wishing it was 3pm so we could be released into the clean outdoors again.

Master Gunn was none the less dauntless in his crusade. Every day he blustered afresh, patrolling the corridors with his head held high, no doubt to escape the pong emanating from cloakbays, toilets and changing-rooms. He had a keen nose, and that keenness was his scourge.

When he retired, a tyrant filled his shoes. Master Maloney was a maths teacher whom I'd had the great misfortune to encounter during my first months in the 'big school'. He made it obvious from the start that he did not appreciate my lack of understanding in maths. Regularly he would demonstrate his displeasure with a well-aimed blow to my head of the type that made my hair stand on end and sent hair slides and glasses skittering across the floor. I often suffered the indignity of having to get down on all fours to retrieve them.

In fact he possessed all the qualities of Master Bradley: he was cold, harsh and unfeeling. And, like Bradley,

Maloney preferred to express his ire through the tactile immediacy of the stick or his bare hand.

He was a redoubtable presence, precise in manner and speech, who never wasted energy or time on the frivolity of smiles or small talk. His only pleasure was his cigarette. After a terse exposition of the topic on the blackboard, he'd set us a problem to solve, and retire to his desk for a smoke.

The red Silk Cut was lit and enjoyed with the ease of a voluptuary. There was an integrated flow of unhurried actions: his left hand rose and rested by turns as the smoke was imbibed and expelled into the fraught room.

I had the misfortune to be seated in the front row, under Maloney's stinging stare and the smarting clouds of smoke. I'd sit there wondering what on earth I was supposed to do and knowing that if I asked his help it would simply bring down his wrath more quickly on my head. So I'd toil with the pencil, making a dog's dinner of wretched angles or quadratic equations, and quiver silently until the cigarette was spent.

Fortunately I didn't have to suffer his fury for too long. His appointment to principal excused him from his teaching duties. From then on I'd see him at assembly time and at breaktime, padding the corridors with the stealth of a tiger, on the scent of troublemakers. Occasionally he'd arrest some hapless boy, seizing him by the earlobe and frogmarching the victim into his office for a mauling.

When I look back I am amazed at the barbarousness with which male teachers were allowed to hit little girls. That we were more fragile and felt pain more keenly than boys did not seem to matter. All pupils — defenceless children — were at the mercy of the moods and tantrums of certain teachers, who could not bring themselves to think of their charges as individuals. We conformed, or we paid a heavy price. I remember being slapped brutally and sent outside the door for innocently smiling to myself. On another occasion the same man called me out from the lavatory where I was combing my hair, to belt me several times across the face. This was no more than an exertion of power — and a naked abuse of that power. Is it any wonder that there is such anarchy in schools these days? The pupils of my era are taking their revenge through their own offspring. The dreadful cycle continues.

Maloney punished the females in a different manner from boys. In our case his hand would become a blurring paddle, slapping the cheeks from side to side with unimaginable swiftness, and finishing with that final hair-raising blow to the head. Hair lacquer was the only cosmetic we could get away with using in those days; it was invisible and thus undetectable. Yet no matter how thick you sprayed it on it didn't offer sufficient buffering power against the Maloney swipe. Girls carried big cans of Silvikrin ('strong hold') in their schoolbags, to minimise the damage.

There was cruelty aplenty in the cookery class too. Our teacher Miss Sharp sizzled and bubbled as much as the contents of her saucepans. She hated everybody, it seemed, and loathed me in particular. I was too dull, too plain, and presumably too witless for her, and so she made my life as miserable as she could. What she did to fruit and veg she did to me: chopping, crushing, grating and grinding. After each lesson my confidence lay in the bin with the scraps and the skins and the debris.

Once inside her room there was no escape. She followed my every move and blunder, lashing out at the spilt sugar, the burnt buns, the broken pastry, the stewing pan of custard. I committed every culinary sin imaginable, smashing and burning my way through that horrid lesson.

She had a handful of favourites in the class and the rest of us were on a sliding scale of preference, varying with her mood. Susan was overweight and shy. Mary-Jane was unkempt. Fiona had a stammer. All these beautiful, blameless girls, through no fault of their own, were targets. With hindsight I realise that Miss Sharp, like Master Bradley, probably hated herself and hated her job, and we pupils bore the brunt of this frustration. Nothing we did was right and, on the rare occasions when we did succeed, we never got the praise we so desperately craved.

PE was tolerable because the teacher was understanding and did not feel the need to make me or anyone else an object of ridicule. But I hated the rigour that those sports demanded. I was not a runner or jumper or batter of balls. I was a clumsy, bashful girl for whom even the activity of talking was an ordeal.

The *real* ordeal, however, took place not on the playing field but when the games had ended. I had to change in front of other girls — and nobody, not even my sisters, had prepared me.

My mother had told me nothing about my maturing body. Anything 'down there' was not up for discussion in our house. Breasts and periods came without warning. I had deduced that there must be something terribly wrong with these unwelcome developments and knew not to go asking.

My mother's voice would drop a note or two when discussing any such matters with the district nurse. Mrs Muck-Spreader called regularly for tea and gossip and a good old hour of dirt-dishing, before moving on to continue her gossiping in a house down the road.

'That daughter of Mary Katie's has another bun in the oven. Isn't it terrible she can't conduct herself?'

'Aye, God it's a shockin' thing altogether with these young girls.' Of course the baker (or indeed the butcher or the candlestick-maker) who put the bun in the oven in the first place never came in for criticism; it was always the young woman's fault. This was the era of the lowered voice and raised eyebrows where sex and the private lives of others were concerned.

There were other ominous signs too. If two actors made to kiss on the TV, mother would be out of her seat like a spring-loaded marionette to change the channel before things got too steamy. Then we'd have to listen to a stream of invective that would have made Mary Whitehouse proud.

'You're not watchin' any of that smut as long as I'm here!' she'd cry. 'What's the world comin' to when you can't sit down to watch a decent film but that dirt has to come into it? That TV'll raise the divil, so it will.'

On Sunday evenings we'd have to sit through a succession of boring programmes: *Z-Cars*, *Dr Finlay's Casebook*, *Sunday Night at the London Palladium*, hoping against hope that we'd be allowed to watch *The Tom Jones Show* at 10.30. But now father became the censor. Just as Tom was beginning a gyrating romp through *It's Not Unusual* he'd be on his feet.

'You're not watching that dirty oul' bugger in this house,' he'd mutter, switching off the set — and mother would helpfully suggest that we all get down on our knees to say the rosary.

Even then I suspected that it was Tom's padded 'down there' that caused father to become so surprisingly alert. He was up and off the couch with an unnatural swiftness, not at all in keeping with his character.

On reflection I'm amazed that Irish men and women from that era ever got round to being intimate at all; and the fact that they did — well, is it not a miracle in itself, begod?

My young mind was thus given yet another phobia to deal with: the fear of womanhood; and I muddled along blindly, developing and bleeding in a fog of ignorance. It would be a long time before sex education was introduced in schools.

I recall one occasion when the district nurse made a visit to the needlework lesson to show, with the aid of a plastic doll, how to bath a baby. A lesson or two in the functions of reproduction would have served as a helpful preliminary. We girls might have benefited had we been taught to connect the mysterious menarche with babies — but no, that would have meant letting us into the great secret of *sex*.

The more I wanted to hide from the world the more it wanted to intrude. I felt like an outcast who tagged along after the others, trudging in the wake of all that vivacity and frolic, bullied by exclusion. I longed for the animated lightness that would loosen all my tense limbs, and make me bounce and dash and toss my head back and be careless and untrammelled and free.

But I was not pretty enough to be lingered over, not clever enough for praise; I was kept from both by the weight of fear at home and at school, and rooted in a limbo of self-doubt. It was reinforced in the looks and behaviour of my classmates and again in the eyes of those teachers who either ignored me or disliked me.

I made friends with another cast-off like myself. Catherine was also a farmer's daughter and poor in most things too. She matched my specs and spots with blunt hair and very red cheeks. Neither of us possessed the status symbols necessary for acceptance into the club: furry pencil-cases, diamanté hair slides, an identity bracelet with one's name inscribed. We were plain and dowdy, the products of ignorant fathers and harassed mothers.

But we muddled along as best we could, clinging together like two flailing swimmers in a treacherous ocean, straining and spluttering under the force of the crushing verve and push of the 'happening' townies – the girls from Draperstown. Catherine and I pooled our resources and plodded our precarious way through thick and thin; we were the two clots who sat together, stuck together, ate together, played together, all this innocent unity compounding the felony of our weaknesses. Catherine and I needed each other. There was true strength in that bond; together we held a flimsy kind of power.

Coeducational schools are bad news for girls; they experience the chauvinism and hegemony of the male too early. The less clever boys – and St Colm's had a great many – attempted to camouflage their shortcomings by dominating and intimidating us girls. They swaggered like little sweaty animals of the lower orders, sniffing us out in order to cast lewd comments about our swelling breasts and bums. Those breasts that went unnoticed by my mother became points of intense interest in the schoolyard.

I was 12 and hated the male of the species with a raw and extravagant passion. How could I be 'friends' with such tormenting little brutes? Master Bradley and father gave me pain, my brothers pulled my hair and gave me grief. In my young head the male reared up as a fearful prospect, a figure to be approached with caution. They were capricious, impulsive; hazards that could break in on me at any time and destroy my whole *raison d'être*.

I cultivated the art of becoming invisible, editing my speech and gestures. I longed for my life to be a series of short, still days with the sun and the birds and the clouds and the green unfolding hedgerows: a natural world to grow calm in. I yearned for a world without the sharp realities of home and school, a place to be alone in.

That gathering danger was forever on my mind. It followed me home from school and woke me from my slumber, and sometimes in the night I thought I heard that 'knocking visitor' under the bed.

> The dark was talking to the dead;
> The lamp was dark beside my bed.

I never believed I could enjoy school. Those first four years with Miss McKeague brought joy, but those that followed lowered me into the depths of despair. From an early age there was the unspoken implication that life was not to be enjoyed but suffered. The unhappy adults around me had themselves grown up with this flawed philosophy and so could offer me no alternative.

In St Colm's, however, I was fortunate to have two teachers who would point me in a completely new direction: Miss Henry, who taught art, and Miss Maguire, my English teacher. The one gave me a thirst for language and the other a yen for colour; together they instilled in me a longing to explore those twin creative fields, a longing that's never left me.

English and art were the touchstones that led me into a new and sustaining world of culture, a world I never knew existed. For the first time I was told that I was good at something. Those words of praise and encouragement flowed through me like a benediction. Suddenly I mattered; I was facing the creative in me. Those good women had kindled flames.

In my English class I encountered the poetry of Seamus Heaney for the first time. He was born and raised in Bellaghy, a few miles from my home. The publication of his collection *Door into The Dark* coincided with my third year at school. Suddenly, in his hands, the sublunary became sacred, the monotony of the elements spoke with an astonishing freshness.

> Rain comes down through the alders,
> Its low conducive voices
> Mutter about let-downs and erosions

My farming father became 'an expert':

> His eye
> Narrowed and angled at the ground,
> Mapping the furrow exactly.

And my domestic mother an occasion of handsome endeavour:

> Now she dusts the board
> With a goose's wing,
> now sits, broad-lapped,
> with whitened nails
> and measling shins.

The poet exulted in an environment I'd never noticed before, and burnished otherwise dull images until they dazzled me. I wanted to write like that and had the effrontery, at the age of 14, to think I could.

Miss Maguire was a dark, vivacious beauty whose energy and enthusiasm enabled me to take risks with language. She was daring in her choice of texts. I was both intrigued and unnerved by Shakespeare. The ambition and evil of Macbeth left a lasting impression and showed me what happens to the human heart when lust for power takes hold: a perfect metaphor for the ego's struggle against God. When we got to the night-porter scene and the mysterious knocking, I fancied that it could have been the recently murdered Duncan doing a Great-aunt Rose.

I loved writing essays and sometimes Miss would ask if Uncle Robert (the Master, English graduate and linguist) had helped me. He barely acknowledged my presence, let alone asked what I was up to in school. I was none the less pleased to think that Miss thought he had a hand in my efforts. It was backhanded praise, but praise all the same.

It was poetry, however, that lifted me up and freed me. It was more accessible than the novel; Jane Austen did not inspire me with all her meandering prose. My parents had no interest in novels. I was raised in a bookless house. The *Sunday Press, Ireland's Own* and the *Irish Messenger of the Sacred Heart* were the height of their literary aspirations. When I met the novel for the first time in secondary school its weight and density scared me. Poetry books were brief and eloquent, the pithy distillations of those more extensive tomes.

So I read and reread the evocative stanzas of Heaney, hoping that some of his magic would rub off on me. I began to write my own verse. Up until I was 20 I continued to produce some dreadful stuff I imagined was poetry: pages of rhyming couplets, doggerel which makes me blush even now.

Mother, marvelling at the speed of this prodigious output – and not understanding a line of it – thought she'd reared a genius. She brought a folder of my poems to Mr Heaney's brother Dan, who was teaching me history at the time. Thank heavens he had the wisdom to put her off, saying that Seamus was so busy he rarely saw him. The folder was returned to me, my embarrassing secrets intact. These few lines I wrote in 'Words' sum up the ardency and frustration of those days:

> Symbolic armies are passing
> Through me by the hour;
> Marching in to gather,
> To multiply and father
> A big, violent marriage in my head
> Throughout the day, they are my saviour,
> Collapsing onto paper unprepared;
> And at night in sleeplessness,
> The poem mutes the prayer.

Eight of those 'jingles' have survived in my memory; they rear up at me from the disaffected past, insisting upon a place in my history. Those iambic rhythms and quatrains, although not earth-shattering, had a power all their own.

From Heaney I moved on to Larkin and MacNeice. What need had I for those canting rosaries when I could recite *Prayer Before Birth* and be empowered by it as I tramped the tarmacked road to and from school?

> With water to dandle me,
> grass to grow for me,
> trees to talk to me,
> sky to sing to me, birds and a white light
> in the back of my mind to guide me.

It did not seem necessary for me to understand those words; it was their mystical essence that enraptured me. This was spirituality of another kind, the creative kind. If language introduced me to it then art certainly gave me the freedom to explore it to the full.

In the art class I found I could do other things with my pencil too. In my hand it became more than a writing tool; it was an instrument that lured meaning into colour, line and shade.

My teacher, Miss Henry, was a fine woman: calm, agreeable, well-intentioned, the fixed point in the fear house that was school. She never startled me with barked orders or sudden confrontations. The thought of the art lessons made me happy. In the hush of Miss Henry's room all my panic vanished, and I rejoiced in being freed from the moil of other subjects. I experienced much the same feelings as I had in Miss McKeague's sewing class. I was at peace, felt safe, unconstrained, and worthy. It was as if I'd shed a great burden, or had happened upon a slash of sunlight in a forest, a light that suddenly defined me, gave me meaning, answering the 'who' and 'why' of what I was.

I set to work with my paints and pencils and laboured over the challenges of still-life and real-life models; capturing the blush on an apple skin or pondering the lineaments of a face. My love of words and art sometimes coalesced. I wrote an 'Ode to the Old Masters', and another poem entitled 'One-Man Show', its theme being the power of abstract painting to challenge the viewer.

> All white and serviceable,
> Susceptible to the bulk of us
> Who've never held a paintbrush.
> At equidistant intervals,
> Framed utterances abound
> By someone who prefers to speak
> With paint instead of sound.

Miss Henry spotted my modicum of talent; my mother picked it up and sprinted with it like a relay runner. If I wasn't going to be a poet, then I 'sure as God' would be a painter. And I like to think that I repaid her zeal and, in a modest way, realised her dream.

Finally I had the attention of the only person I truly wanted to please. This nascent talent diverted mother, gave her focus; it made the days timeless and the roads straight. She could see ahead to great things: exhibitions and celebrations; her gilding of all those futures was the spur that urged me on. My creative skill had given her a vicarious kind of fame.

She was my patron and I was the poor beneficiary, a Vincent to her Theo. My new-found ability made her bold. She persuaded father to cut into the housekeeping tranche, using the goad of education and the certainty of picture sales. Suddenly canvases and tubes of expensive oils appeared; and every trip or tour she took was a hunting expedition for postcards and pictures and photographs. They littered the house, all the contextual references I needed for my transforming brush. She would arrive home like a robed Maecenas bearing gifts; a spill and rush of objects that would bring those visions to life. No canvas I painted could disappoint her. She overlooked flaws clearly visible to me. Love broke out and bloomed in her. With that brush in my hand I was faultless. All those sweaty fistfuls of posies I'd plucked and carried home to her from primary school, in a bid for her attention and a smile, were now being repaid one hundredfold. I painted the 'mantelpiece candy' that she adored: scenes of rural tranquillity that demanded nothing but bribed the eye and attempted to beat the camera at its own game. I painted mountains, lakes and dwelling houses, all in their proper places, and all augmented with the vivid hues of fantasies and farce. These renderings of the landscape were the language she understood.

I painted on request, for the doctor and the dentist and the neighbours down the road, and she sold my canvases at such bargain prices that I rarely obtained a decent return. Mother excused the injustice with: 'But we couldn't charge too much; sure she's a friend,' or 'He's your teacher,' or even 'She'd be a second cousin of the parish priest, you know.' She loved conducting these transactions, delivering the finished product into the buyer's hands and carrying back to me the measly profit and the effusive praise.

She also knew how to put those WI ladies in their place. Some of them had the impudence to suggest that the paintings were too good to be done freehand and that I must have painted by numbers instead.

'For goodness sake, Avril,' she'd sniff, 'numbers are for amateurs!' She said this, knowing that certain ladies in the WI group — Avril included — painted by numbers as a hobby.

My love of painting almost made school bearable. Those days when I had art lessons were the best of all. They filled me with such joy that not even Miss Sharp or the bullying boys had any power over me. My creative imagination was let loose to float in whatever direction I chose.

THE WEIRD AND THE WONDERFUL

My experience of the artistic was developing through the poetic image. I began to observe beauty in the commonplace as I trudged to and from school with my brothers Mark and John.

I began to sense an energy that riffled nature to new heights. The wind breathing through the trees; greens variegating from dark to light; a fence with the snagged wool of sheep on the barbs; the swell and fold of the Sperrin Mountains shifting under the sun; purple foxgloves straining proudly; a dazzle of windscreens; the glitter of raindrops on ferns; a fence post rotting at a tethered gate; wet leaves varnished on the road. My heart expanding, my eyes truly seeing for the very first time.

I knew I irritated my brothers when I'd stop continually to study an unusual piece of foliage or the play of light on a bramble.

'What's keepin' ye?' John would say. 'Would ye hurry up, would ye? Sure it's only an oul' bush!'

On wet days we took the bus. The features of this area of Ballinascreen were less arresting than those I encountered in my earlier days, no doubt because we used the main road between Tobermore and Draperstown. At that period, in the early seventies, quite a number of families who didn't work the land had moved from the rural areas to the newly built council estates in the town.

The old-style shacks that had accommodated the likes of Jamie Frank and Great-aunt Rose would soon become the deserted relics of a long-flown time; fallen tombstones that spoke their ghostly histories through crumbling walls and broken doors.

The road was ours no longer; there were more cars and buses than ever before, so we traipsed in single file, tramping on one another's heels and standing well into the hedge when we heard the thunder of a lorry. There were few Mary Catherines to detain us. But, to compensate, we had the weird and wonderful Norrie.

Norrie was a transvestite — though at the time I was unfamiliar with the term. To me he was simply a man who liked to 'walk out' dressed as a woman. Given what I now know about those less enlightened times, I realise that Norrie was fearless. He was also polite, happy and inoffensive — or a 'harmless cretur', as my mother used to say.

The gossip fingered Norrie's mother Maggie as the architect of this situation. She wanted a girl child and, on giving birth to a boy, could not accept him. She thus condemned the infant Norrie to years of frilly boyhood and the adult Norrie to a life of long-line bras and scent. I'd see them at close quarters on the late bus I sometimes took from school. Maggie made a brash statement without speaking; her face was a powdered mask of panstick pink, her hair as black as a raven's wing. She swelled out of high heels and tight frocks, carried a handbag in front like a Highland dancer's sporran. Being a teenager, stilettos and handbags interested me greatly. Once I peered into the gaping mouth of Maggie's bag as she paid the bus driver. Inside I saw a collection of surrealism that would have inspired an entire Dali series: a make-up bag, a pension book, a pair of worn tights, a pound of pork sausages, an upper row of dentures and a clock.

Since Norrie lived just a couple of fields away from us, I had the opportunity to observe him at close quarters. His daywear collection consisted of 'safe' biscuit-coloured separates: a belted raincoat, polyester slacks, a buff-coloured handbag and matching Scholl sandals. He wore a felt beret to conceal his baldness and a powerful amount of slap and powder to conceal the traitorous evidence of a razor.

In fact, if you'd sat him down in a hip London nightclub, he could easily have passed for the artist David Hockney, similar glasses and beret being the Hockney signatures at the time.

This bland mode of dress in public was deliberately adopted to neutralise the impact of his cross-dressing. On seeing Norrie for the first time you tussled with the dilemma of how to pigeonhole him — not quite a man, but then again not really a woman.

Most of us hate nonconformity; we judge and label and box everyone we meet in order to still the panic that sheer eccentricity can bring. Norrie knew this all too well; consequently he dressed 'down' in public so as not to cause offence, and 'up' in private when all those judgemental eyes were looking the other way. The Norrie I'd observe through the meadow gate when idling on a Sunday afternoon was not the colourless figure who shared those bus journeys from school. He'd have emerged from the drab chrysalis of that dowdy raincoat and metamorphosed into an exotic butterfly that shimmered and flitted within the safe confines of his garden.

His summer collection — his 'private' wardrobe — looked as though it had been put together in a darkened room by a myopic seamstress. Norrie would parade about his garden, committing every sin in the fashion bible. There was a crêpe-de-Chine frock in a furious cadmium orange (I knew my palette now with all that painting); a satin blouse with fearless flounces rampaging everywhere down the sleeves, round the cuffs and opening onto a hairy chest. He favoured preposterous shoulder pads, long before Nolan Miller put them on the dames in *Dynasty* and *Dallas*. There were skirts of the floaty, pencil and A-line variety, and all finished with pairs of stilettos that looked even higher than the Yankees'. Polka dots fought with checks, and violent reds screamed at timid pinks. This was courageous dressing at its best — or worst, depending on which side of the fence you were leaning. Norrie could have shown those staid ladies of the Women's Institute a thing or two.

Often on lazy Sunday afternoons his mother and he, emboldened by the sun and sparseness of the traffic, would stroll out to the end of their lane, and venture onto the public highway, or the 'county road' as we called it. Those were acts of bravery. On these occasions Norrie would camouflage his baldness with a brassy, blonde wig or shelter under a straw hat the size of a griddle. At a distance, with the light behind him, he looked positively female. A short-sighted motorist would not have suspected a thing.

I also used to see him shopping in Draperstown with his mother on Saturday afternoons. In my early teens those trips to the town were the highlight of my week. Morose and silent as usual, father would taxi mother and me between the shops. First the grocer, Mr Kelly in High Street, where she bought the flour and tea and sugar and whatever other basic foodstuffs were needed. Her purchases were always basic.

The shop had shelves going all the way up to the ceiling, filled with tins and bottles and packets of every description. It was a fascinating panoply of colourful labels which took my eyes for a walk and relieved the boredom of having to listen to those adult conversations. There were bottles of Camp coffee and Sanatogen wine; tins of Birds custard, and Ovaltine and Horlicks which mother sometimes bought to help her sleep; there was Persil washing powder and big yellow cakes of Sunlight soap.

A door set into a section of the wall opened onto the hallway of Mr Kelly's home. Both door and wall were festooned with various items of haberdashery and first-aid. You were not aware of this gap, until his wife would come in through it, creating a magical breach and setting all the dangling zips, plasters and whatnots in motion.

Mother would read from her list and Mr Kelly would fetch the items. Often he'd have to climb a ladder to reach the otherwise unreachable, his expert hand plucking the products from the shelves. As he stretched and leaned outwards I'd giggle to myself, thinking he resembled a skilled monkey up a tree.

He wore a snuff-coloured shop coat and always had a pencil lodged behind his ear. When all the groceries were assembled on the counter he'd free the stubby pencil and lick its tip. Mother always asked the same question.

'What's the damage, Hugh?'

And he'd proceed to tot up the bill, mumbling to himself as his eye roved over the purchases and mother stood waiting for the bad news.

Our next stop was the butcher for the Sunday cut. I didn't go in there because I hated having to look at all that dead flesh, too visceral and too malodorous for my young sensibilities.

The last stop was Burns's clothes shop, which I loved. It smelled of new fabric and fine leather and its long, cool interior stretched itself around a corner on two levels. It had counters polished to a high sheen, used mainly for measuring and cutting cloth. This shop was the final gasp of the Drapers Company, set up all those centuries earlier. The rails of overlapping garments were mustered in ranks and files, the more expensive items swathed in protective layers of cellophane. The shoeboxes were stacked to the ceiling and labelled to correspond with size and sex.

Upstairs in the ladies department mother would chat to Miss Quinn, the elegant assistant, and try on whatever coat or dress caught her eye. Miss Quinn was tall, slim and perfectly groomed. She had long nails and long eyelashes and I knew my mother — who was probably not much older — felt like a dud beside her. I was in total awe of this lady. She replaced the Yankees in my head, holding up a picture of polish and refinement that I dreamed one day would be mine too.

I'd linger among the rails of clothing while mother fitted on various 'costumes' and covertly watch Miss Quinn touch up her lipstick. Sometimes she'd catch me peeking and would flash me a smile; I'd quickly turn away, feeling guilty, and gaze out of the window at all the hurrying Saturday shoppers.

Finally the curtain would swish back and out mother would come, looking proud in the chosen outfit. She'd wheel and shift in front of the large mirror, her head going this way and that, advancing and reversing as the praise flowed from the assistant.

'Mary, it's lovely,' she'd hear. 'It's really you, just perfect for your colouring and dark hair.'

And mother would smooth down her stomach and say: 'Are you sure it doesn't make me look fat?'

'Not a bit of it,' Miss Quinn would lie glibly, lifting a finely arched eyebrow and adding helpfully: 'But if you want I can let you have the latest Playtex eighteen-hour girdle at a good discount.'

So mother would muse and flirt with the idea, a conflict of figures and desire and what-would-he-say going on in her head. She'd always err on the side of caution.

'Oh, it's lovely, Anne,' she'd say with a tinge of sadness, 'but it's too dear; I couldn't afford it. He would go mad if he seen it.'

And Miss Quinn, being kind, and eager to make a sale, would bat in with that well-aimed sale clincher.

'Nonsense, Mary! Don't worry about him or the price. Sure you can put a deposit on it and pay it off.'

And with that mother's mind was settled, the deal was done. Miss Quinn would expertly tear a swathe of brown wrapping paper from a roll by the counter, fold the garment into a neat parcel and secure it with a length of string. Mother would give that 'to hell with it' smile as we left the shop. I knew she was experiencing that rare and sudden rush that comes with blatant misbehaviour.

She bought most of what we wore in this way, paying in instalments, making the odd purchase for herself which she'd hide from father's disapproving eyes until she found the appropriate occasion and time to wear it.

Now and again, especially at sale times, I'd see Norrie and his mother in the ladies department, rooting through the lingerie. Norrie couldn't try the items on — for obvious reasons — and you were greeted with the bizarre sight of him holding up in front of his chest a succession of bras and slips. All would be done as quickly and furtively as possible, and all for his mother's approval.

Burns's shop provided me with some prize items which made me feel very special too. Those communion and confirmation frocks, a green coat with a shiny buckle which I adored, and a pair of patent-leather shoes which were so beautiful I could hardly bear to wear them. I kept them in their box under the bed and, if I felt sad or bored, would take them out and caress them, standing them on the tissue paper to admire. Those shoes were only for wearing on very special occasions.

After these Saturday forays we'd like as not arrive home to find one of our neighbours on the doorstep: John Mallon, who regularly ceilidhed on a Saturday night.

John was a sober bachelor, just like my uncles. He wore a long serge coat, in dubious black – the colour of choice for the wifeless man, since it didn't show the dirt and therefore excused the need for care and attention. Like Robert's raincoat it covered a multitude. Even on stiflingly hot summer evenings I never once witnessed the shedding of that weighty coat. He accessorised it with a pair of matching wellingtons and a cap that bore the lustre of a decade's wear or more.

John Mallon's modes of transport were rather unusual – not least because the demands of driving a car had obviously proven too great and forced him to adopt inferior, and rather imaginative, alternatives.

He had a Bella scooter to begin with, the very poor relation of Eddie's BSA. It was a beige-and-maroon affair and it heralded its slow approach with a long, low, thrumming note. That unusual yet all too familiar sound on a Saturday evening never failed to bring all us children to the window and mother to the edge of despair.

'God,' she'd complain, 'it's not that John Mallon again – coming on a Saturday night, of all nights, when I haven't a wain or a stitch washed for mass! Me heart's a breakin'; I may give this place up.'

But there he'd be, making his gradual approach on the Bella, the black coat winging out leisurely at his sides. In the twilight glow of those summer evenings he could have passed for an overweight Count Dracula (if you can

imagine Dracula in a flat cap). His generous frame
dwarfed the little bike so much that it appeared as though
he moved towards us under some supernatural
propulsion.

From the Bella he graduated to a bubble car, a curious
little vehicle; it had a windscreen that looked like the
bulbous eye of some intergalactic monster. This three-
wheeler was steered by handlebars, had a large, front-
opening door and a top speed of 35mph.

It was designed and built in 1953 by one Ernst Heinkel,
the man responsible for the Heinkel-III bomber. The
story goes that after the war the Germans, their struggle
having ended prematurely, were left with a surplus of
forward turrets from their Luftwaffe bombers. In the
interests of economy they employed Mr Heinkel to come
up with a solution and his answer was the bubble car. It
was in production for four years, after which time the
Germans sold the design to Dundalk Engineering in the
Irish Republic — and so it was that Mr Mallon acquired
his Heinkel bubble car.

Of course I was unaware of its history back then. John
used to give me a lift from school in this contraption
which, even as a child, caused me great embarrassment.
I was not to know, as I sat in the bubble watching the
hedgerows gliding past, that the humble plexiglas dome I
gazed out of might well have soared above the cumulus
and borne witness to the fear and fury of some hapless
RAF fighter pilot as he screamed his way towards
eternity.

On stopping in our yard John would raise the car door
and emerge from his bubble like a chick hatching. He'd
ceilidh for a good hour or two, dispensing the stories
and latest gossip of the day. In winter he carried an oil
heater in the little car and would transfer it indoors on
arrival. This heater was as weird looking as the bubble: it

was a large, round dish-like affair — much like today's TV satellite-dish — with a tiny, red mantle at its core. John would sit at the roaring range with the heater strategically placed between his legs (central heating of another mode entirely) and discourse with father at length.

Their tedious conversation was the remit of all the visitors to our house. There were no heated discussions on Darwinian principles of natural selection here, I'm afraid; no debate on the importance of Cocteau's contribution to European modernism, or even Kandinsky's influence on abstract expressionism in the 20th century. No, sadly there was little to send my imagination rampaging down new thought-provoking paths.

What I got instead from father and Mr Mallon went something like this.

Mallon: 'Saw a son of Johnny the Digger's up on the brae face with a brand new tractor and a buckrake this morning. Aye, a brand new one, no less. The gleam of it would damn near have blinded a body, so it would.'

Father: 'Boys a dear, is that the nixt of it? They've a lot a call for that, sure there was nothing wrong wi' the wan they had.'

Father rarely approved of anyone spending money. In his book farm machinery especially should last over several lifetimes.

Mallon: 'Aye, ye know what's wrong with that crowd? Too much ground under them. Sure them young boys are not content unless thir rippin' and tearin' and roarin' the guts outta cars and trucks and God knows what else. That tractor got fierce abuse, so it did. No wonder it didn't last.'

Mr Mallon made the noises father liked to hear. Extravagance and the follies of 'young boys' were favoured topics.

Father: 'Aye, ye may quet the craic. There were less new tractors in my day, I'm tellin' ye.'

Mallon: 'Now you're talkin', Mark.'

Then mother might weigh in.

Mother: 'Saw Josie the Digger at mass last Sunday. She's a trig blade, Josie, so she is. Hat on her the size of a cartwheel. Johnny doesn't mind spendin' a bit of money on his wife, I'll say that for him, John – not like that man in the corner.'

John, not wanting to get embroiled in a marital dispute, would counter.

Mallon: 'Now, Mary, you'd look well in anything. Josie the Digger needs all the help she can get. No matter how much paint or powder, begod, even if they hung the crown jewels round her there'd be no difference.'

Then poor Josie's physical appearance would come in for a mauling.

Father: 'Funny lookin' head on that Josie wan.'

He'd lean back on the couch and wait for the prompt that would allow expansion and a laugh from Mallon.

Mallon: 'Has she now, Mark?'

Father: 'Aye. When she's walkin', the head's way bobbin' out in front of her and the rest of her's comin' behind. You'd think somebody was pullin' her on a bloody lead, so ye would.'

Mallon: 'Aye, she's in a wile hurry to get first to the altar, y'know.'

Father: 'Couldn't she sit at the front then? Save all that runnin'.'

My mother would then attempt to stick up for her sex again.

Mother: 'Josie wants to show off her nice clothes, y'know. That's why she sits halfway down the chapel. And I'd do the same if I had Josie's finery, John. But there's not much chance of that. That man'll not spen' a ha'penny, so he won't. You know how copper wire got invented, don't ye?'

Mallon: 'How's that, Mary?'

Mother: 'It was when two of them McKenna brothers were fightin' over a penny between them, and neither would give way.'

Mallon: 'Boys a dear, Mary, that's a good 'un!'

John would laugh loudly and father would look sour.

Father: 'Sure clothes niver made anybody. What's a lock of oul' pallions for anyway?'

Mallon: 'Only for covering up the naked truth.' (More like the dirty truth in Mr Mallon's case.)

Father: 'Now you've said it, John.'

And they both would laugh and John would clap his hands for emphasis, bathing in the afterglow of his own wit. He couldn't bear those irksome silences that followed as the laughter died, and would whistle through his dentures and contemplate the ceiling as he riffled through his memory for fresh fodder. Inevitably, if all else failed, he'd come up with a subject that guaranteed enough mileage and mirth to keep the pair of them going until morning: our neighbour Mrs Potter.

Elizabeth Potter, a widow in her early seventies, was the cause of many wagging tongues in the locale, largely because she didn't fit in — and, in a place like Ballinascreen, that would never do. She was the sister of Mary Catherine, the spinster-angel on the great bike, she who plied the roads and prayed for all. Mrs Potter disowned her. She'd left the area and gone to the USA, where she married a wealthy man. On his death she'd grown homesick and returned to her birthplace. But while Mary Catherine dwelt in her lonely little cottage, Elizabeth resided in what she referred to as 'my beautiful bungalow', entertaining the neighbours and ignoring her sibling. My mother was sometimes invited to Elizabeth's soirées, and I was allowed to tag along. We weren't invited in the interest of generosity or friendship but more in the spirit of showing off to the yokels Mrs P's sense of style and how things should be done.

The bungalow had been specially built to her exacting specifications, and was bedizened with the tat of her travels. As a child I was transfixed by the bric-à-brac that crowded every surface and room in the house. The gallimaufry in Helen's place wasn't a patch on this. There were ornaments and figurines of every description everywhere: maidens, angels, fairies, dogs, cats, soldiers, dolls and teddy bears, fashioned in every material imaginable. Mrs Potter was like a latter-day Miss Havisham, surrounded as she was by the detritus of childhood, trying vainly to preserve the memories of that lost innocence through this welter of trinkets and knick-knacks. Touching any of them was strictly forbidden, which was difficult for a child like me, having been raised in a house devoid of such trappings.

Mrs Potter was eccentric in her manner and had a peculiar way of dressing. She sagged in out-of-season separates, wore ganseys with frayed elbows, skirts whose hems fell down at the front and rode up at the back, exposing mottled flesh and stocking-tops. Her shoes, cracked and down at heel, had angry upturned toes. She wore what looked like a tea cosy for a hat.

Meeting her for the first time you got the impression of casual, slovenly eccentricity, but she immediately doused such ideas with her gimlet eye and cunning manner. She burned with envy and bad faith; spread sweet praise like icing-sugar in public, chopped everyone to pieces in private. 'Lord in heaven, Mary, that Biddy McStay is intolerable.' I was afraid of her and would quail at the very sight of her, scurrying off to play or hide when she came to visit mother. She had the same effect on me as did Uncle Robert.

Soon after the acquisition of that beautiful bungalow, Mrs Potter bought a brand-new Mini Cooper, a status symbol in the late 1960s, much in the manner of today's BMW. Mrs P, however, bought the car before securing her driving licence, which proved rather an oversight. Being advanced in years, she was sorely tested by motoring. She lacked concentration and aptitude, and her eyesight was poor. Driving lessons were needed, and she ended up spending a small fortune on them. It was rumoured that her instructor was able to build an extension to his house and purchase a second car on the back of Elizabeth's incompetence.

She finally realised her ambition on the sixth attempt. John Mallon, ever the sceptic, claimed that she had bribed the examiner, which may not have been too far from the truth. I can just picture the frustrated inspector sitting beside the calamitous Mrs P, conscious of his worsening odds in the mortality stakes and thinking to himself: I cannot endure this another time.

In short she was to driving what Norrie was to the fashion industry: a magnificent disaster. For whatever reason, Mrs P had decided unwisely at 72 to take her life in a whole new direction, steering haplessly towards a world of fearsome gear shifts and shuddering hill-starts. Some of her takeoffs from our yard were spectacular events — much more enjoyable than Eddie's motorbike. We'd stop our play and watch the Mini buck and jump for a good five minutes before suddenly shooting off like an out of control lawnmower. Mother warned us not to accept lifts from Mrs P, no doubt imagining the prospect of having to arrange a funeral. And on our leaving for school she would caution that if we saw the widow coming we were to stand well into the hedge. We took her advice to heart. At the sight and sound of that ominous Mini we would scramble for the safety of the grass verge and wait until the 'killing' machine had passed.

Often on our way home from mass we'd see the stranded vehicle by the side of the road, where Mrs P, having experienced yet another 'unexpected difficulty', had somehow found the extraordinary courage to abandon ship.

She provided John Mallon and father with a reservoir of gossip that never ran dry. The bubble car and Mini had had a number of near hits it seemed. So they'd drink the compulsory tea and blether about her to fill those lulls. They verbally ravished the neighbours with the ferocity of lions round a carcase. The wives and spinsters of the parish were the frail flesh they fed on before moving on to gnaw the more pithy hearts and bones of their fellow males. Father was an expert vitiator. No one escaped him.

Global events never featured in their talk. A nuclear bomb could have dropped on London and no one would have noticed. As I listened to those conversations I was given to understand that everybody except my father was deeply flawed. Such negativity cried out for a counterbalance; I found this in my art.

Three Days in Purgatory

Mother was so proud of me in 1975 and I was mighty pleased myself. I'd sat my GCSE exams the previous year and now I earned the distinction of being the first pupil of St Colm's to sit and pass an A level in art. Mr Maguire, my one-time Latin teacher, had now become principal, and it was thanks to his confidence, my art teacher's faith, and a shaky belief in my own ability that enabled me to pass it. This pivotal qualification was the springboard that would launch me into a completely different world and land me within the esteemed walls of the Belfast College of Art.

Mother was jubilant. Finally her prayers had been answered and my talent confirmed.

I was rewarded for all my hard work in a most unusual way. I had hoped for a few days' vacation in Portstewart, but it was not to be. I did get a few days away — not in Portstewart, however, but in *Purgatory*.

My mother, being the devoted beggar of favours from on high, and rarely experiencing the bounty she desired, looked on my A-level success and subsequent admission to art college as a miracle.

She thus reasoned that it was a miracle which demanded thanksgiving of a special kind. A few token rosaries on bended knee would not do — Lord, no. Instead she signed the pair of us up to endure a gruelling, three-day stint in St Patrick's Purgatory, Lough Derg, County Donegal.

Station Island, as it is commonly referred to, has been a centre of pilgrimage since at least the 12th century. Tradition holds that the good man sojourned there for a time yet there is no hard evidence to support this. The so-called Tirechán history puts him in the district of Donegal around the year AD 700. So it is possible that Ireland's patron saint sought the solitude of one of the lonely caves on the lough in order to pray and do penance.

The island is a plateau of forbidding rock rising out of the still waters. It boasts an impressive basilica with a copper dome — and at that point sadly the grandeur and glamour of St Patrick's Purgatory ends, as I was to discover during my short captivity.

This basilica started life as a humble church, built in 1780 on the site of the caves where St Patrick is said to have prayed. The imposing structure which stands on the island today is the culmination of many years of construction and artistic endeavour. There are just three other buildings on the barren rock: a small chapel, a dormitory for the pilgrims, and the priests' quarters.

One can still see evidence of the Celtic monastic period, particularly in the 'penitential beds'. And it's in these penitential beds that the true meaning of Purgatory is revealed.

'Bed' is hardly the term I would use. These circles which inflict so much pain are the remains of monastic cells, or oratories, where monks passed their days and nights in solitary prayer and contemplation. They are rings of boulders and rough stones embedded in the soil, some at a steep incline; in the middle of each circle stands a crucifix. There are seven in total, each of their names commemorating a saint connected with the Donegal area.

From Draperstown to the island is a 70-mile journey and mother and I travelled the first leg by coach. We had a morning start, so early that it made our WI excursions seem genteel by comparison.

Johnny the Digger (remember him?) had organised this trip. He was a large, pious farmer who wore braces and a belt, which was a wise precaution, given his girth. He was obviously in sympathy with his fellow Kerry farmers who find those twin supports necessary too, 'just to be sure, to be sure, begod.'

When I think about it now, I believe that Johnny, at some earlier stage in his career, must have contemplated the priesthood, rejected it — and spent the remainder of his life regretting that decision.

How else to account for his passion for doing good deeds for the Church and organising pilgrimages to focal points of devotion? There was Knock, Croagh Patrick, and Station Island, they being the most popular ones in Ireland. The Digger was a dedicated and fervent church layman who took his duties very seriously indeed, that repressed ambition of his being ever to the fore. Not content with allowing us the peace and relative calm of the journey before the purgatorial storm, he would launch into the rosary at every available opportunity. We must have said six in total, with him swaying up and down the aisle, bouncing off seats like an inflated buffalo, and roaring out the decades with some choice pronunciations of those sainted words.

'Blissed art thou among wimmim!' he'd bellow. 'Forgive us our trispisses; and Sacred art of Jezis we place allertrust in ye!'

Whenever he detected a drop in pace or volume in our mumbling he took it as a sign of flagging zeal and blasted out the decades with so much ardour that even the bus windows rattled a response. I was hungry and tired (we'd been fasting from midnight) and now my head was beginning to throb with the Digger's litany.

It took us over two hours to reach the island. The last leg of the journey was to be by water. When I saw the sodden-timbered boat I suddenly regretted having given in to mother. But I put aside my fear and joined about 90 others, and together we were steered across the lough to whatever it was that awaited us.

Lough Derg actually means 'red lake' and refers to the blood of the last great serpent Patrick is said to have slain. There was an urban myth abroad in the 1970s – and, given the superstitious nature of the Irish, probably still has currency – that if a red-haired woman happened to be sharing your boat then the chances were high that it just might capsize and drown you. The belief sprang from the only notable disaster of this nature; it occurred in 1795 when a vessel carrying 93 passengers sank just a short distance from the quay at Station Island. The only survivor was one very fortunate red-haired lady.

Mother and I were rather anxious in the light of this knowledge. Little wonder: among those we knew making the pilgrimage was a friend from my primary school, red-headed Marie. There were lots of anxious faces on that crowded boat when the innocent Marie stepped aboard. I reckon it was the only occasion when people actually prayed that they'd make it to purgatory rather than meet their end beneath the churning waters of a lake.

Not for nothing is Station Island referred to as St Patrick's Purgatory. Upon landing, you surrender your shoes as well as your right to proper sustenance during the following three days. You also relinquish your right to sleep for the first 24 hours. This ordeal is clearly not for the faint-hearted and, after the first day, I began to question how that joyous A level could have brought down such affliction on my head.

The island was crowded with misery-makers chanting endless rosaries while making circuits of those woeful 'beds'. There was a timetable of hardship for us to follow: something like 54 rosaries a day to be recited while circumnavigating each of the circles in turn. We paused twice daily for a single cup of builder's tea — black of course and sugarless — and a slice of dry toast. There were also oatcakes which looked and tasted like compressed cakes of hamster food. I discovered on the first day that one nibble was enough to set my stomach on a protest race, in both directions; so toast tasting like cardboard it had to be.

My poor mother, God help her, was up for it all. She went at these duties with the diligence and fervour of a drill sergeant second-guessing the whims of an inspecting general, and made very sure I complied with every part of the ritual.

Then there were the feet. Hunger and exhaustion were bad enough but the sight of so many naked feet caused me pain as well. I never realised how dainty and inoffensive my own were until I encountered the variety of monstrosities stumbling about the island — a pedicurist's nightmare, or a chiropodist's dream.

Having endured enforced insomnia, delusional hunger — I swear I kept seeing Mars bars and French Fancies — and a brain-numbing headache that intensified with each passing hour, I wanted to throw myself into the lough and thrash my way back to sanity. My mother on the other hand took all this hardship in her stride. She smiled and prayed and loved every minute of it. But then she'd been toughened by so many years of hardship.

I could see that this suffering was not so much emotional as physical. Such pain is easier to deal with because it puts the powerless in direct touch with their own, bounded realities. They can see the blood and bruises, and that is joyous; it makes them feel part of the universe. Mental pain is intangible and cannot be so easily displayed. On Station Island the 'offer it up' principle, which characterised the Church's stock answer to my mother's suffering, was given a somatic vocabulary for all to see.

We underwent an all-night vigil in the 'Prison Chapel' — the name says it all. Outside we went, renouncing the Devil resoundingly with outstretched arms. Round and round we went, even if it rained, even if it snowed, buffeted by the wind and the sharp awareness of our sinning selves: praying, praying, praying.

Inside again to the relative warmth of the basilica. Up and down the aisle and nave we went, in single file like prisoners in an exercise yard, invisibly shackled by rosaries, sleeplessness and hunger, chained together by decade after decade after decade. Until at last the awakening sun fell through the stained-glass windows, bathing our heads in light.

The following day I staggered about, as if I had just survived 24 hours in the desert. All moisture pulled from eyes and mouth, my head throbbing. I was simply aching to stretch out on the nearest bench and sink into oblivion. However any attempts at sleep were quickly thwarted by a hearty priest who went about prodding those he saw were about to nod off. There was no escape; I'd just have to endure every bitter minute of it. Meanwhile my valiant mother soldiered on, performing her painful duties, striking her breast, bowing her head, kissing the cross, and desperately whispering her entreaties to God.

At ten o'clock on the second night paradise did indeed come, in the form of a bunk bed and a single blanket. I let mother have the bottom bunk and I collapsed into the top one. Only a set of drab canvas curtains separated us from our neighbours. It seemed that I had slept two hours at most before a bell started clanging outside the cubicle. I peered through the curtains, to see a termagant in green overalls; to the accompaniment of this unmerciful racket she was urging us out into the keen air of dawn. I had the sinking feeling that I'd just woken up in Lowood Charity School; at any minute Mrs Scatchard would haul me out by the hair to suffer a humiliating harangue from Mr Brocklehurst. Instead I got my shoes — my delectable shoes! — handed back to me and sat down to a Dickensian farewell breakfast in the refectory hall. This was to be our final day of purgatory.

Elation swept over me at the thought of release. I could not quite believe that I'd come through the torture. After a final round of the island we departed at midday, my mother ebullient and proud and I exhausted and sick. God had been well and truly thanked and, with the staunch devotion of the time-serving egoist, I kept telling Him that I was due a big favour in return for my sacrifice.

At War with Colour

When I went to art college in 1976 I walked away from raised voices in cluttered rooms, endless rosaries on the cold floor, my father's anger, my mother's pain, my easel under a skylight in the garden shed. And walked towards the violence of Belfast and the freedom of a flat, a goodbye to religion and money in the bank, platform boots and braided hair, Paul Simon on a turntable beside my bed.

I knew that I wanted to paint from the moment I first held a brush in Miss Henry's art lesson. None the less my artistic training started with a foundation course in all the visual arts: I sculpted, threw pots, took photographs, printed fabrics, designed a handbag and even soldered a necklace. After a year's exploration of all these areas I emerged knowing what I'd suspected all along: that my desire to paint had not diminished despite my hands coming to blows with all those other media. I was so looking forward to my degree course in fine art.

I imagined the prospect of those art lessons with Miss Henry being stretched over a three-year period — painting all day and every day — and I could barely contain my excitement. However my dream was short-lived. The Ballinascreen painter, with her naive aspirations and notions of art, was to encounter the avant-garde ideas that obtained in the fine-art department — and be thrown to the wolves.

The Belfast College of Art is a glass building given over to creative endeavour. Its unimaginative, many-windowed design is a poor imitation of the Bauhaus style of architecture perfected by Walter Gropius in the late 1920s. It sits at the far end of the city's main thoroughfare and, because of its location, suffered and saw a good deal of the political turmoil that ripped through the heart of Belfast in the 1970s.

My college life coincided with these 'troubles'. I was witnessing the authenticity of some of those Eddie Bradley stories, but certainly not to the extent that bullets were whizzing past my ears; nor was I dodging bombs on a daily basis. The Provisional IRA, having despaired of ever reaching a compromise or solution with the British Government and the corrupt, single-party state that was Northern Ireland, had embarked on a bombing campaign. Their targets were British and Unionist installations, army personnel and police officers – or 'legitimate targets' as they liked to term them. The bomb, however, being an undiscriminating weapon, made everyone a 'legitimate target', often killing or maiming passers-by.

Living in the city at that time was therefore tense, but not so disabling as to make me want to run back to the shelter of my home in Draperstown. The police and army were apt to search you on the street. They also had the power to detain you for as long as they thought fit, to check your identity and credentials. You therefore felt uneasy at the sight of them and would try to be as inconspicuous as possible so as not to catch their eye.

I was adept at making myself seem invisible. Who would have thought that the school-yard bullies could have taught me something useful after all? There were also many irresponsible and vile acts of terrorism carried out in the name of freedom. Carrier bags containing explosives were left in crowded restaurants and shops without adequate warning. Such hazards necessitated your handbag having to be searched every time you entered a shop. After a few months, being questioned by the authorities and searched by security personnel became routine.

There was, however, a glimmer of light in the uneasy darkness of that time. In August 1976 the Women's Peace Movement — later called the Peace People — was formed by Betty Williams and Mairead Corrigan. The group called on the women across Northern Ireland, both Protestant and Catholic, from the 'working and idling classes', to come together in the interests of peace and reconciliation. They demanded a woman's right to 'live and love and build a just and peaceful society'. The brave voices of those two women were heard, but not heeded as it turned out. It would take 18 more years of bloodshed before the men of violence woke up to that sane message from the women of peace.

So I entered a Belfast that was hopeful at that time, and I viewed the occasional inconvenience as a risk worth taking if I were to pursue my studies. My love of painting and my desire for freedom heavily outweighed the negatives. For the first time in my life I had been released from the prison that was home and was experiencing the independence that goes with being a self-governing adult in a grown-up world. If that meant living in a war zone, I reasoned, then so be it.

I shared a flat with another student whom I'd met on the foundation course. Margaret was a composite of Doreen and Catherine from my schooldays: a tall, calm girl whose tranquillity made me feel anchored and safe; our unassuming natures drew us together straightaway and emboldened us in the face of all the posturing pretension that surrounded us. We conformed to some extent. We wore our platform shoes and modest denims and moved among our limp-wristed sisters, who were all got up in what looked like the result of frequent and desperate traipses round the Oxfam shop. Later on I daringly crimped my long tresses as some kind of necessary compromise.

The two-bedroomed flat we shared was a bleak little dungeon situated off the Antrim road; it was not the most salubrious part of Belfast. Travelling to and from college Margaret and I would see the women of the neighbourhood, shuffling — slippered and rollered — to and from the shops, fags hanging from mouths, tabloid newspapers rolled up like batons, engaging with the harsh reality of another day. No, we'd chosen the flat not because of the charm of the area — or its interior design — but because of its proximity to the college.

It was owned by a shark who posed as a landlord by day. And by night? Well, who knows? Margaret used to remark that there was 'something of the nightclub about him', what with his shiny ties and teddy-boy sideburns. Mr Shark became another ominous figure to add to my growing rogue's gallery of villains.

Our flat paid homage to his thrifty nature; he did not believe in throwing things out. Everything in the place had its lifespan stretched to screeching point. No piece of furniture was ever allowed to go quietly into that good night. Father and he would have got on famously I fear.

He was a miserable, exacting man — face frozen in sharp angles — for whom it seemed food and smiles were luxuries he could ill afford. He came on the twenty-eighth day of every month to collect his rent and would stand in the doorway, one bony paw extended, and wait, wordless and grim-faced, while we ferreted for the cash. On one occasion we were late with payment, and arrived home from college to find our humble belongings bundled into several bin-liners ranged on the pavement. We never forgot the rent money again.

The living-room, where we conducted most of our life and leisure, was devastatingly drab. The walls, carpet and couch were all rendered in swirling shades of 'uplifting' orange and brown. The two armchairs had been ruptured beyond endurance so that when you sat down it was a breath-heaving struggle to get up again, like trying to free your arse from a bucket. The windows were small and grubby and further deadened with greyish bolts of nylon.

In the evening this depressing scene was lifted into sallow relief by a shadeless, 25-watt bulb. Mean Mr Shark didn't allow anything stronger and we didn't dare defy him in this regard.

Thus did I live for three whole years. I don't think it's unfair to say that if one felt ambivalent about committing suicide then Dunneyfield Park, off Cliftonville Road in West Belfast, might well be the place to persuade one into making the ultimate decision.

One of the advantages of youth, however, is that it blunts you to hardship — hardship whose severity can only be appreciated in retrospect. That awful flat never looked or seemed depressing to us then, simply because we were living independently for the first time and therefore had no yardstick. Sadly the same could not be said of our initial experience at art college. During my first week on the course I began to question the sagacity of my fine-art choice and the sanity of some of my tutors.

One in particular, an Englishman named Alex Wilde — a *senior* lecturer, mind you; that did not bode well — certainly believed in living up to his surname at all times. There were 30 students on the course and our first assignment was entitled 'Reality in the Room'. Each day we were locked into one of the studios with only our art materials, and asked to interpret the title's meaning in our own way.

The room had been stripped of its contents; there was no furniture, no pictures, no points of reference other than a radio that had been tuned to white noise. We were also instructed not to speak to one another — which was very difficult, given the jaw-dropping dramas that unfolded during this incarceration. Let me explain.

With each passing day something truly bizarre would take place, usually orchestrated by Mr Wilde. On one particular day we were sitting idly sketching each other when suddenly the door burst open and in strutted a strange man wearing lederhosen and a blonde wig, his hairy legs bristling with excitement and his ungainly feet stuck into a pair of frail stilettos. He made Norrie look like a nun.

He pranced around the room like a catwalk model and halted temporarily, as models do, with one hand resting on his thrusting pelvis, elbow flapping almost Uncle James-like, and his left foot shoved back at an obtuse angle to help steady the provocative pose. Who knows, he might well have been attempting to mime an easel, but I could not make such 'creative' connections at the time. Here I was fresh from the bogs of Ballinascreen, with my very limited palette of experience, being asked to interpret what can only be described as sheer madness.

In the evening, in the gloom of our sublime living-room, Margaret and I tried to make sense of this strange performance but drew a blank. We consoled ourselves with a Vesta Paella and a Findus savoury pancake enjoyed while watching *Crossroads*, both hoping that the reality of the following day would never come.

But Alex had something entirely different in store for us that day. He'd evidently decided we needed some calm and entered the room dressed soberly in black trousers and sweater. If the garb was reassuring, however, his actions were anything but. He was armed with a toothbrush and a dustpan; harmless enough items, you would think — until Alex went into 'crazy mode'. He spent the entire day sweeping the dust up off the floor with the toothbrush and heaping it into neat piles at different points in the room.

After three days my sketchpad contained nothing at all of interest, just a few doodles of those stilettos. The other students were equally baffled — with the exception of a few secretive weirdos (and they are on every art course) who seemed to be engaged in their own, frantic renderings, work they refused to share with the rest of us. The truly mad are a selfish lot.

And abruptly, on the penultimate day of my confinement, inspiration came. It came from a most unexpected quarter. The door to our prison opened timidly and a slim, young woman entered. I guessed she must be a latecomer to the course. I was mistaken. She began to saunter round the room, slowly discarding her clothing, until finally the pale, stark truth stood before us.

As a callow country girl recently released from my rural moorings, who'd spent her schooldays hiding her girlish charms and unaware of, shall we say, the more prurient side of human nature, I was gobsmacked.

I spent the next hour quelling the shock by drawing the model; it would have been highly insulting to have ignored her. Stripping off in front of strangers cannot be easy for any rational woman, regardless of the context. The reality of that crazy room had finally propelled me into action.

At the weekend I went home and recounted the experience to mother. She reacted by crossing herself several times and saying that the devil was loose in Belfast. Father wondered what the world was 'coming to anyway, anyway, anyway', and concluded in his ever-positive manner that I should 'come out of that hole'. It must have been a tremendous disappointment. My parents had spent most of my youth 'editing' TV footage of kissing film stars and gyrating pop singers, yet here was the decorous Belfast College of Art giving me a crash-course in gratuitous nudity, in my first week undoing all my parents' work of moral counselling.

In the end, however, mother got a mass said for me and we mumbled our way through an extra rosary just to be sure, to be sure. And on my departure for Belfast on the Sunday evening she soaked me with enough holy water to drown a Jesuit. I would have to stay the pace — and drive out Old Nick into the bargain.

Yet as the course progressed I began to see the reasoning behind the lunacy of that inaugural week. We had all come to college accustomed to the rigid demands of our A-level course, knowing our palettes and perspectives to the last hue and line. That was art of the head; now we needed to engage with the art of the soul. That bizarre room with its jolts of senseless action was the catalyst we needed to set those safe perceptions on a more scandalous and revolutionary path.

My safe 'mantelpiece candy' had to go. At first I was reluctant, and fought against the bohemian ideal with a perfectly manicured canvas; this was despite my tutor's instruction to delve into my own Self instead of miming the trite narrative of the camera that any monkey could imitate. I refused. He in turn refused to acknowledge me, and I sat for three weeks in a wilderness, wondering how it was that my dream of being the perfect painter could have come to this.

After the despair and tears I got angry and cut up my canvas. I rearranged the fragments, intending to paint the disruption. The result was an abstract work of disquieting beauty which moved and amazed me. I had managed to actualise my passion and distress; the noetic had lost out to the inspirational. With this move I got the immediate attention of my tutor and stepped over into the compelling and enriching world of abstract expressionism.

As the weeks passed, those photographic images of my earlier years became a dim memory on a distant shoreline as I pulled away in my unsteady boat. I was powered by emotion and necessity to head towards the maelstrom of raging colours and soaring lines that would transcend all representation and give me 'pure art'. That exhilarating journey would never end because I was experiencing my destination through its unfolding. My spirit was speaking to me for the very first time. My paintbrush became my guiding force.

It was both exciting and unnerving to discover all this. For the very first time, from beneath all those layers of disorder, I was unearthing another reality, another self, an inner self I never knew existed. Here was my coded diary in riotous paint, the dull entries of a conflicted life given vivid testimony which had the power to pull spectators in. I found that there was nothing more rewarding than being able to paint in this way. You presented the viewer with the challenge of having to interpret *your* message in *his* own way. No two people can have the same experience when they look at an abstract painting; they have to struggle to find meaning. That's why the bourgeoisie will invariably choose the chocolate-box image; it's safe, it's easy and above all forgettable.

So out went my anodyne landscapes. I abstracted my way from the serenity of those mountains and lakes, the mute vases and bowls of fruit, the lifeless portraits and cute cats. I crushed and milled the very essence out of them, to sweep form and colour into totally fresh directions on the canvas. My love of poetic lyricism found its way into these compositions, too, as I struggled to become accountable for every mark I made and every pigment I used. I was coming to realise that, just as poetry was the quintessence of language, abstract expressionism was the quiddity of pure painting.

The more eager I grew, the more my output increased as I tried to paint myself to new heights of discovery. My canvases became bigger — the extreme being 6' x 4' — and bolder, and more intense as time passed. As the poets of old sought inspiration in absinthe so I was trying to paint myself towards the definitive canvas; I sensed that at some point in the future (I did not know when) I could back away from the ultimate masterpiece, with brush in hand and the answer — in all its persuasive glory — before me.

Oh, the passion and fury of those days! I began to understand why painters sometimes go mad. They glimpse infinity through the lens of the paintbrush and attempt the impossible: to try to capture it all in a single lifetime.

The poetry of MacNeice and Heaney was now replaced by the spiritual visions of Paul Klee and Wassily Kandinsky.

Born in Russia in 1866, Kandinsky is considered to be the father of abstract art. He first studied law before emerging as one of the most original and influential artists of the twentieth century. He was also an accomplished musician as well as a deeply spiritual man. A spiritual lawyer? Now there's an interesting juxtaposition to conjure with! At 30, Kandinsky gave up law to study painting. It turned out to be a very wise move.

I was heartened, during my studies, to discover that his introduction to abstract painting happened in much the same way as my own. Upon seeing one of his figurative works lying on its side on the easel he was struck by its beauty, a beauty far exceeding that manifested by the canvas when upright. So moved was he by the abstraction he saw that he set about painting the 'emotion' of that experience. The result was the birth of abstract expressionism, a movement that was to change the direction of art in the early years of the last century.

Kandinsky's paintings carry the emotional power of a musical composition. In fact he asserted that he heard music in colour. 'Colour is the keyboard', he stated. 'The eyes are the harmonies, the soul is the piano with many strings. The artist is the hand that plays, touching one key or another, to cause vibrations in the soul.'

So Kandinsky became my inspiration and my mentor during my college years. He caused a revolution in my head. As he had painted through his love of music, so I was attempting to paint through my love of poetry. The poetry I'd written — trite as it was in those early days — was my spiritual message, and I worked to get across in paint that spiritual part of me. My fear and confusion swirled and collided within the confines of every canvas, while at the same time freeing me from the limits within myself.

Running parallel on this frantic journey of discovery was the slow evolution of my own personality. Margaret and I were not party girls. We had yet to become acquainted with the liberating effects of alcohol, so we rarely got invited to the bars and discos of the student's union.

Truth be told I never felt part of that artistic coterie; it required you to chatter endlessly about the reasoning behind your work and pontificate on the trends and influences that appeared to be of the utmost importance to you. Surely art should make its own statement without having to be explained. Often in the art studio those wise words of the Buddha came to mind: 'Only speak if you can improve on silence'.

I loved art but hated the pretension. It usually followed that the bigger the ego the more mediocre the work and the more convoluted the discourse to justify it. Quite a number of very good students did not get the recognition they deserved simply because they weren't voluble enough. Nor did my own reticence endear me to those hip tutors. So with very little instruction from any of them I attacked my canvases, fighting my silent war, using brushes and paint as my weaponry.

It came as no surprise that my mother's reaction to the new 'abstract' me was not favourable. She couldn't understand any of my canvases and I knew it was pointless trying to justify what she chose not to understand. She blamed those mad tutors at the college for ruining everything. So for her sake I did not become a complete turncoat, and continued to do her commissions at the weekends and at holiday time.

Whenever I had a free day from college she liked nothing more than to take the early bus to Belfast to shop. She'd stop off at a supermarket on the way, and arrive at the dingy flat bearing enough food to keep us going for a month.

She'd have dressed up for these occasions, and usually wore her favourite dress: the yellow one. This garment was all the more precious because she hid it from father. It was too bright, too expensive, too good to be true and too wicked to go unnoticed, so she'd conceal it under her dowdy raincoat until she left the house. Once aboard the bus she'd shed the coat along with the deception. She was sunny and carefree at times like that, taken out of herself for the day and heady with the thought of freedom and escape.

Mother, like most women, had what she called her 'fat' days and her 'thin' days; today we call them bingeing days and dieting days. Those visits to Belfast were more often than not of the fat variety, as she threw caution and that Playtex girdle to the winds and feasted recklessly. And I was the all-too-willing fellow conspirator. We'd have a sugar-rich 'Eddie Bradley' breakfast with perhaps a slice of scarcely thawed cheesecake thrown in. We were like naughty schoolchildren left unsupervised. For her it was release from drudgery; for me it was freedom from college for a day. After the gorge we'd pile onto the nearest Citybus and head for the clothes shops.

Marks & Spencer was my mother's favourite. She never seemed to tire of exploring its clothes-rails, with me checking the size and price of any garment she fancied. Then it was into the changing-room and I would wait for her as I'd done all too often in Burns's shop — my words of blandishment at the ready — waiting until she emerged into the light. At lunchtime we'd eat our way through another mound of food, washed down with — very daring! — a glass of house white.

Mother lived for these excursions. For a whole day she was free of her vituperative husband. She felt buoyant and took risks, eating and buying what she wanted, before being reined in again to the drudgery of being a country housewife. She was eating and spending to dull the ache of that drudgery, while at the same time praying to be released from it.

She probably realised that release would only come through that most ultimate of departures. For now she'd make do with these snatches of happiness, holding on to them like pools of essence in her hands, the inevitability of their transience enabling her to keep at bay for a while the sorrow of letting them go — just for a little while.

I sensed her fear too, that undercurrent of foreboding that tugged at the most innocent of rituals, made me realise how unworthy she felt, and confirmed the same feelings in me.

I could glimpse it in her face and in her actions: at the bus-stop getting the fare out of her purse too soon; in a restaurant putting up with inadequate service; in shops not asking the assistant for a receipt when it was forgotten. She never wished to incur displeasure, in case she drew attention to herself. She was afraid to engage fully with the world and to take her rightful place, because no one had given her the acceptance she was entitled to or the validation that should have been hers. The Church had rendered her practically powerless and father had finished the job.

As mother tried to pray her way out of her distress, I painted, sublimating pain with my paintbrush. Those days at art college were important inasmuch as they focused me on my emotional incompleteness, and created a need in me to explore and search for answers.

JOHN HENRY AND THE MALTESE BROAD

In 1979 Margaret Thatcher became Britain's first woman prime minister; the newly elected Pope John Paul II visited Ireland, and I graduated with an honours degree in painting from the Belfast College of Art.

I also became aware of a far more important qualification I needed to study for, and one which would serve me better than any piece of paper. To acquire it I knew that I must travel beyond the accepted standard of what I had become, to apostatise the dogmas that had reinforced it. I knew in short that, in order to see the light beyond the shadows, I would have to piece together meaning from the fragmented truths and fictions I'd grown up with.

That year will also be remembered for less laudable events. On 27 August Earl Louis Mountbatten, the queen's cousin, was killed by an IRA bomb at Mullaghmore, County Sligo. A few hours later the tranquillity of the beautiful seaside town where I once lived was torn apart; the bombers had struck again, slaughtering 18 British soldiers at Narrow Water, one of Warrenpoint's most picturesque spots.

On 30 September the pope addressed an audience of 250,000 at Drogheda in the Irish Republic and made an appeal for an end to violence in Ireland.

> To all of you who are listening, I say: Do not believe in violence; do not support violence. It is

not the Christian way. It is not the way of the Catholic Church. Believe in peace and love, for they are of Christ. On my knees I beg of you to turn away from the paths of violence and to return to the ways of peace. You may claim to seek justice. I too believe in justice and seek justice. But violence only delays the day of justice. Violence destroys the work of justice. ... Do not follow any leaders who train you in the ways of inflicting death.

Two days later the IRA responded to the Holy Father. 'Force is by far the only means of removing the evil of the British presence in Ireland,' they stated. 'We know also that, upon victory, the Church would have no difficulty in recognising us.'

Such arrogance in the face of righteousness! Yet it is true to say that men who create war do not live by the laws of a higher power but by the selfish dictates of a lower one: their own ego.

My days in Belfast's war zone were numbered however. My last summer holiday from art college ended with my graduation day. In many respects this day resembled my First Communion, but I'd swapped the white frock for a black robe and the artificial piety for real pride. My mother and brother John came to witness my big moment.

Father could not be trusted to behave himself among the academic elite; we were sure he'd go out of his way to embarrass us. I had visions of him challenging the strength of one of the tables at the post-reception buffet, sending the food to the floor and us into hiding.

Our fears were not entirely groundless. Just such an incident had loomed at Helen's wedding when my parents were guests. Mother was alerted to danger by the sound of shivering cutlery, and saw the wedding cake leaning at an angle to rival the Tower of Pisa. She found father in the nick of time, crouched by the top table, examining a leg joint.

So my graduation was father-free and therefore risk-free. He couldn't have cared less anyway. When asked if he'd like to attend, he responded with the evasive enthusiasm that characterised his whole life.

'Naw,' he said sourly, 'I'll not bother me head.'

That this occasion would be a one-off event did not seem to impact on him. He was not a man to mark the success of his family.

He was as predictable as the seasons that he never tired of commenting on. My landscape paintings would be held up for his approval, and rejected one by one. The skies were too blue, the mountains too flat, the houses too big, too small, too this, too that. Early on I realised that it was impossible to win his favour, and simply gave up trying.

Mother was forever the go-between, smoothing the way and trying to keep the peace. She ignored his criticisms and was so proud of my achievement. In the end that was all that really mattered to me.

This time around, thank heavens, she did not suggest Station Island, Lough Derg, as a reward for all my efforts. Instead I got something far beyond anything I could have imagined: a three-week holiday in California. We were off to visit my Uncle John, mother's long-absent brother whom she had not seen in 33 years.

Her five brothers were the complete opposites of my father's family. They were kindly, light-hearted men, who had gone out and engaged with the world at an early age, doing backbreaking work to sustain themselves while following whatever youthful dreams they had. Unlike the

McKenna boys' situation, there were no pots of money or acres of land to detain the Henrys at home, or stanch the course of their lives until death took the parents and delivered the goods.

The two youngest, John and Peter, had emigrated to the United States in their early twenties. Dan, Frank and Paddy had married, raised families and, like mother, chosen to remain close to their roots.

Dan was the uncle I came to know best; mother and he were very close. His calm, endearing personality showed me how mother could have been had she not come under father's baleful influence. Being in Dan's company was like being near a warming fire; he melted any reserve you might have, and brightened your spirits with compliments and praise you felt you didn't deserve. What I never heard from father I heard from him; Dan's generosity of spirit made up for the shortfall. I was always told I looked well, even when I didn't, and given smiles to lift me when I was down. Truly spiritual people are a rarity. Uncle Dan had achieved his serenity through an effortless acceptance of himself. There were no masks or barriers, no rigid viewpoints to be strenuously defended, no need to be always right. He had managed to subdue the ego so that his spirit was fully alive. The memory of his humility has left a lasting impression on me. He was living proof of Emerson's belief that 'the best effect of fine persons is felt after we have left their presence.'

So I was looking forward to meeting Uncle John. Mother had a fund of stories about the devilish young prankster. He had been the joker of the family, the life and soul. His CV was impressive: he'd left home at 17 to work in a factory in England. From there he travelled to Australia where he stayed for a year. On his return home he discovered he couldn't settle and set sail for

America with little money in his pocket but big ideas in his head. He worked his way across the Land of the Free and finally settled in Sacramento, California, where he married a Maltese-Canadian by whom he had three children. John had always promised mother that he'd visit Ireland, yet she knew he never would. If she were to see him again she'd simply have to bridge the distance herself.

Quite naturally mother wanted to look well for her brother, and that meant dieting. She had a month to lose a stone and knew from experience that willpower was not always enough.

She therefore enlisted the help of her GP, who prescribed for her a course of slimming pills. In reality they were amphetamines, and were very successful. She lost the weight – but she lost sleep as well. She soon developed a non-stop urge to continue talking and working into the small hours. I used to hear her at four in the morning, washing and hoovering and singing to herself, a tornado in a housecoat, capable of amazing feats, sweeping all before her. She might have been going crazy but the pounds were falling off and her self-esteem was rising. John Henry would see a svelte Mary after all.

The pills worked, that is certain. Just how effective they were was shown to me at a rock concert at Slane, County Meath, later in the year. I observed the ageing lead singer of a headlining band leaping round the stage for a full two hours with the energy of a ten-year-old. I suspected where that lean energy might have come from: mother had it in a bottle under her bed.

The countdown to our departure began, and she still wasn't losing the weight fast enough. A sweat suit seemed the answer. As long as there are overweight people wobbling about this planet of ours there will be no end to the gimmickry that is peddled with the empty promise of a quick-fix, minimal-effort solution. Mother's sweat suit was one of them.

She bought it by mail order from the back page of a Sunday supplement, believing the dubious claims of the snake-oil merchants that you could lose ten pounds *while you slept*. Each night she retired to her bedroom looking like a Soviet cosmonaut, ponderously moving down the hallway before climbing into bed to sweat. In fairness, the pounds did disappear but I fear this was due entirely to water loss. After several cups of coffee she'd have regained it all. I didn't dare tell her this of course. She was very pleased with the result, convincing herself that the 'needless' expenditure was worth it, and I willingly colluded in the fraud to keep her happy.

We were unused to air travel, mother and I, and the journey to Uncle John's home was a gruelling one for us: ten hours in total with a night transfer in New York. We finally arrived exhausted, legs and feet swollen like figures in a Beryl Cook painting. At Los Angeles we changed in the airport toilets, re-applied our make-up yet again, trying vainly to cover the cracks of that sleepless journey. Mother donned her yellow dress for this very special moment; we walked out into the hazy Californian sun and waited to be claimed.

John Henry ran from nowhere with arms outstretched. Even after all those years he'd no difficulty in recognising his sister. They embraced for what seemed a long time, shedding tears of joy in the full realisation of that landmark moment. It was a moment they never believed would come. I looked at this tableau of reunited siblings and knew I was witnessing the acme of my mother's life. It was the happiest she had ever been – and would ever become. There was nothing left for me to do but aim my Pentax and shoot that amazing moment.

John was 55 when we met and mother six years older. He was a jaunty, agile little man, fully alive to the moment, a coruscating presence who 'dressed smart' and 'talked quick'. And boy, just like those Yankees, he could talk!

With his thin moustache and glinting specs he could easily have passed as an understudy for Sir John Mills. He'd prepared for this occasion with care. He was dressed in a dapper, nautical outfit: navy-blue, brass-buttoned blazer, white slacks with matching shirt and loafers, the ensemble finished off with a red silk cravat, and a crimson handkerchief that spilled out of his breast pocket to add a rakish note.

He drove us to his home in a gigantic Oldsmobile saloon, he and mother sitting way up front. I travelled in the rear, dwarfed by that vast interior, rolling from side to side like a pea in an empty suitcase. I thought of John Mallon's bubblecar and mused idly that if Mr Mallon were put behind the Oldsmobile wheel he might well believe he was at the controls of a Boeing 747.

John's driving encouraged me to think that he had probably attended the Mrs Potter school of motoring. The car bounced and floated over the road as he regaled mother with rapid-fire commentary on the sights that unfolded, casually negligent of adherence to the Highway Code. He'd brake suddenly following yet another near miss, stick his head out of the window to holler 'I pay my road tax too, you gaddamn bastard!' while mother crossed herself and I curled up into an even tighter ball. I never fully appreciated the usefulness of seat belts until I travelled with John Henry.

We finally arrived at the house, exhausted, distraught and extremely hungry — we hadn't eaten for hours — and concealed our discomfort lest we cause offence.

We were introduced to the 'Maltese Broad', John's moniker for his wife Carol. She was waiting for us on the lawn together with the children. They had two sons and a daughter, who grinned and gushed the requisite words of welcome before scampering off to do more exciting things. I was not much older than them yet felt like a pale old dud beside all that tanned, handsome vigour. I wanted to join them but there was no invitation so I reluctantly retired with the adults to the air-conditioned coolness of the house.

The Maltese Broad was a large, sweet lady who spent most of her time in the kitchen 'fixing' food. Unfortunately she bore the evidence of this obsession all too clearly, and mother was thrilled to discover that by comparison with Carol Henry she was a mere Twiggy. The irony was that both John and his wife were so excited with our arrival that they forgot to offer us food. This was an occasion for celebration and we felt obliged to accept the whiskey and Budweiser on offer; we ended up merry as well as famished. Eventually, about six hours later, with John getting more animated and voluble with the help of Jack Daniels, we repaired to a Chinese restaurant for that longed-for meal.

The couple made up for it, however, in the course of the holiday. Each day was a re-run of that introductory day, but with more food than our bellies could handle. Our consumption was gross and unseemly; this was every Christmas and birthday multiplied by 21 and squared to the nth degree. During those three weeks we were never again allowed to feel the hunger pangs of that first day.

Every morning we'd rise to find the Maltese Broad in the kitchen, flipping and tossing onto plates the raging contents of a skillet. We picked up the jargon pretty quickly because Carol talked of little else: eggs over-easy, hash browns, gammon rashers, crêpes suzettes with maple syrup, cornbread, potato cakes. I'm sure there was an endangered species or two in there as well. This was coronary thrombosis on a plate.

And all the while we were shovelling and glugging, John Henry fizzled about — I was certain that carbonated blood coursed in those veins — making more noise than the frying pan. He was recalling the old days while cutting his coffee with copious sloshes of whiskey, halting sometimes with an empathic, 'Jesus, Mary!' or 'Gaddammit, Mary!' He'd lament the decline in morals in the USA: 'Those gaddammed Beatles ruined this country, Mary!' He'd get down on his knees and thump the floor to hammer home a point while mother and I sat looking on in wordless astonishment and Carol kept the food coming.

The food! It seemed that no sooner had we finished eating, gone to the loo to freshen up than we'd come back to find another charge-laden table waiting. There was no such thing as humble elevenses of tea and a biscuit here, I'm afraid. The table would groan under the weight of bagels and cream cheese, Oreos, muffins, cookies and buckets of chocolate-chip ice cream with toffee sauce. In retrospect, mother's speed-induced, sweat-suited diet was a fortuitous preparation.

In the evenings we dined out. John would don his nautical outfit and Carol would waddle in his wake, wearing spandex leggings and a dayglo smock which only just concealed her burgeoning hips. She was not a rare sight; most of Sacramento seemed to be populated with enormous people who resembled bouncy castles, and wobbled and undulated under tent-like structures that passed for clothing. Mother and I kept staring in amazement, but no one else seemed to pay them a second glance.

John drove us in that mighty saloon car of his, swearing and swerving over the highway, making eye contact with us instead of the road. Miraculously we arrived at each destination with our limbs intact.

If I didn't know better I'd swear that John had had assertiveness training at the School for the Insecure Irish-American Male Approaching a Mid-Life Crisis. No sooner were we in the door of a restaurant than he'd start to vandalise the silence and complain about the 'gaddamn service'. These exchanges followed a pattern I began to recognise.

Waiter: 'Hello, how are you, sir ... ladies.'

John: 'We're pretty damned good, as a matter of fact, but this table ain't.'

Waiter: 'Pardon me, sir. I'm real sorry, sir, I'll see what I can do.'

John: 'You sure as hell better. This is my sister Mary and her daughter, who I ain't seen in thirty-three years. You got that? Thirty-three gaddamn years! And they've just flown six thousand miles from Ireland to see me. And we ain't gonna sit with our backs to the view in the middle of this restaurant like some gaddamn monkeys in a cage. We want that table by the window, you hear, and we want it now.'

And he'd point to a table already occupied by a couple tucking into their steaks and fries.

Mother and I would sit red-faced, curling our toes in the silence that followed. We were not ones for causing a fuss in public. The waiter would stand there glaring at us and we knew what he was thinking; it was all *our* fault. Sometimes mother would feel moved to intervene.

Mother [*whispering timidly*]: 'The table's all right, John.'

But John was having none of it.

John: 'Mary, we ain't sittin' at this second-rate table and if things don't start to improve round here pretty gaddamn soon I'm callin' the gaddamn manager.'

A hint of urgency would enter the waiter's voice.

Waiter: 'Yes sir, I understand, sir. We'll see what we can do.'

We'd be ushered into the lounge for complimentary cocktails and the waiter would approach the couple by the window. They'd invariably move to another table without question. We were to learn that the Americans are uncommonly obliging to their Irish cousins. I could not imagine the same scenario in an Ulster restaurant.

Those meals out were generally served on 'platters' as opposed to plates. The steaks were so thick that it seemed only an acetylene torch could cut them. There were mountains of fries and vegetables. I may be exaggerating but I seem to remember washing everything down with gallon beakers of cola and litre glasses of wine. Dessert was considered compulsory rather than optional, so we helped ourselves from the trolley. Again the American idea of pudding was not what we were used to. We could choose from belly-heaving portions of pecan pie, chocolate flan, apple strudel, cheesecakes, trifles, gâteaux with melting heaps of ice cream in every conceivable consistency and combination. There was creamy thick, double creamy thick, double creamy, creamy thick, and the unimaginable, extra-double-creamy-thick, in blueberry, chocolate chip, toffee, strawberry, and on and on and on. It appeared that everyone in the restaurant — ourselves included — was engaged in some kind of eating marathon, heads down, elbows working like pistons.

I consumed so much I could even feel my head getting fat. There was no end to these bacchanals. When we finally got home and struggled into the house the Maltese Broad would stagger off to the kitchen and re-emerge bearing platters of bedtime snacks: pretzels, peanuts, corn chips, potato chips and a host of dips and relishes. I'd collapse into bed and remain comatose until morning — when my senses were assaulted by the aromas and sounds of Carol doing what she loved best: fixing breakfast.

Halfway through our vacation John took us to his place of work: the offices of the *Sacramento Bee* newspaper, where he was employed as a printer. The *Bee*, I learned, had quite a colourful, proud and impressive history. Perhaps no one exemplified that more than its founder, James McClatchy, an Irishman and great-grandfather of the present publisher.

After emigrating from Ireland in 1840, McClatchy became a writer for the *New York Tribune*. But the lure of the California gold rush drew him west in 1849. He boarded a ship to a Rio Grande port, crossed Mexico on foot (that's right, on foot), was ferried up the coast, walked 300 miles to San Diego, then made his way overland to Sacramento.

After disappointing results in his quest for gold, he returned to journalism. McClatchy was clearly a man of great resource and enterprise; the McKenna brothers could have learned a thing or two from him.

He died in 1883, leaving behind a newspaper that today serves an area of approximately 12,000 square miles, covering most of Northern California.

All these facts and more besides were related to us by a public relations officer for the company, Errol T Johnson, an impressive Denzel Washington look-alike whose duties included guiding visitors around the *Bee*'s offices. John felt we needed to be fully briefed before we met his co-workers. He was also very proud — and rightly so — of his employer's history and achievements.

Mother and I, hung over and bloated from the night before, followed Denzel around like a pair of sheep, nodding and feigning interest.

Denzel: 'The *Bee*'s combined average circulation totals one point four million daily and one point nine million Sunday editions.'

Mother: 'God save us!'

Denzel [*looking puzzled*]: 'Yes, ma'am. We're a newspaper that has a rich history of standing up for human rights and engaging with environmental issues. In the eighteen-sixties we took a strong stand against slavery and voiced adamant opposition to the Ku Klux Klan.'

John: 'Remember those gaddamn bastards, Mary? Wore those pointy pixies with the eyes cut out. As bad as those sons-a-Protestant-bitches back home. Them Protestants ruined dear old Ireland and those goddamned Beatles ruined *this* country.'

Mother: 'God, that's terrible, John.'

John: 'Tell you something for nothin', Mary: there'll never be peace in good old Ireland till the Provos whip those gaddamn British asses the hell outta there.'

And he was off like the clappers of hell. Denzel patiently checked his gold watch and adjusted his tie while he waited for John to finish his rant on 'gaddamn British imperialism'.

Denzel: 'The courageous voice of the *Bee* was heard again in nineteen twenty-two when it published the names of Sacramento's Klan members — including prominent citizens — in a front-page exposé. Such fearless reporting has earned the *Bee* twelve Pulitzer prizes, three of which were coveted gold medals for public service.'

John: 'You hear that, Mary? Twelve Pulitzer prizes and three gold medals.'

Mother: 'Heaven's above, John, that's a terrible lotta prizes. He was a great man that McCracken. Where'd you say he was from?'

Denzel: 'McClatchy, ma'am. From Lisburn, County Antrim, ma'am.'

We were then shown the rusted typewriter which James McClatchy carried all the way from County Antrim in pursuit of the American dream.

So that was John's impressive place of work: a vast skyscraper full of 1,800 busy bees, all living up to the title of their product. And he was determined to introduce mother and me to each and every one of them.

We started in the basement with the raw grease and inked-up rollers of those gigantic printing presses, and ended 50 floors later at the advertising department, marvelling at the suavity of the designers and copywriters.

Virtually every employee knew John and addressed him by his full name, John Henry. When I come to think about it, it seemed more fitting than plain, dull, monosyllabic 'John'. He was so full of life that only his full name would do. I can't remember the many people he introduced us to but the routine went something like this:

'Hi, John Henry, how are you? You're lookin' pretty sharp/neat/swell/good today.'

'Why, thank you, Vern/Bubba/Marylou/Clarisse. I'm pretty good, as a matter of fact. May I introduce my sister Mary from Ireland, who I ain't seen for thirty-three years?'

'Gee, John Henry, that's awesome.'

'And this is her daughter, the poet and artist Christina McKenna.' (I was really chuffed to be described in such terms.)

'Well, I'm mighty pleased ta meet ya all. You have a nice day, y'hear.'

We grinned and gripped more hands in one day than the Queen of England. I now know how she feels at the close of yet another state occasion. All evening the echo of that introductory mantra went round and round in my head. John Henry made sure we missed no one.

He was so proud, tugging those cufflinks into view, smoothing down the silk cravat and hankie, the two high notes of that nautical ensemble. He was reminding himself that he was no longer the humble employee but a jazzy showman and we his guest soloists.

Appearances and impressions were important to John Henry. He paraded us as exotic extensions of himself, one Derry lady on each arm; we danced to his tune, being reasonably pretty and decorous, and he made sure everyone in that building saw us.

We went to Reno, Nevada, to try our luck at the tables, and visited casinos that were thumping insults to modesty and good taste. Waitresses paraded in the skimpiest costumes and most of the men looked like small, medium and large versions of Sly Stallone, replete with the chest rug and medallion.

There were ladies of all ages and sizes, and others who looked suspiciously like the Sunday variant of Norrie of Ballinascreen. There were good-time gals with improbable bosoms who'd been stitched and tucked in all the right places. They lusted for the attention that had once been effortless, clinging on to the last vestiges of sex appeal by their fiberglass fingertips. But it was the elderly dames who intrigued me most: vigorous old bats with wind-tunnel face-lifts, their withered throats and wrists shackled with jewellery; juicing the last drops out of life before the inevitable fall. They attacked slot machines with a cold anger, thumping them when they failed to cooperate and cursing like navvies. John swore they could hog a machine for the entire day, feeding it dimes and dollars in the mad hope of scoring that elusive million; those face-lifts had to be maintained.

Such places gave insanity a whole new meaning. This was Dante's fourth circle of hell with tassels and beads — the antechamber to hell's last bawdy-house. I could sense mother's lips move in sibilant prayer and knew the sign of the cross was certain to follow. Sure enough, I caught her in that very act more than once.

There was a message here for all Irish pensioners. Don't spend your final years clocking in old people's homes, gaddamn it! Get out of there and buy a one-way ticket to Reno or Vegas and live dangerously at the tawdry gaming machines, in crackpot paradise. I could picture John Henry doing just that a few years down the line.

Our visit to the States was intoxicating. Indeed, it was more intoxicating than we'd imagined. Halfway through our stay we wondered why we were still suffering from jet lag. The explanation was bizarre. Mother and I had made initial forays to the supermarket, when we managed to escape from John. On one such expedition we discovered a wonderful, sweet-tasting milk with which we liberally doused our cereal and coffee each morning. We'd even finish off with a generous glass or two of the stuff, just to keep us going. We thought there must be something in the air because often after breakfast we'd stagger to the bedroom with barely the energy to get ready, never mind go out for the day's excursion.

I cleared up the mystery on the tenth day of our stay. Idly scanning the label of the 'milk' carton one morning, I discovered we'd been drinking piña colada at 37° proof! It came as an almighty shock to realise that we'd met John Henry's colleagues and his many friends, and experienced everything through a drunken haze. We'd blamed the plane journey, the weather — we'd even suspected Carol's cooking — before learning the 'staggering' truth.

Thereafter we reverted to sober old milk and the days didn't seem to be half as much fun. At the same time those days in California were the best of my mother's life. The fleeting joy she had experienced on those shopping trips to Belfast had been stretched across three luxurious weeks. She walked taller, her laughter was louder and her smiles wider. With her brother John around, the sun never set and the darkness didn't have the nerve to fall.

I will always remember John as a quick, restless little man who shot words like bullets, ran at life like a prize sprinter, jumping over the days, kicking all those 'gaddamn' obstacles out of sight. America had made him bold, eager for tomorrow, hungry for change; the bigger picture always beckoned, the never-ending possibilities of a wide, unlimited future.

Only my mother could make him stop and take a breather. I'd hear them well into the night, John reclaiming the past from a shuffle of memories that only the drink and nostalgia could call forth. He had never returned 'home', preferring to remember Ireland through the eyes of the young man who had left all those years ago — the picture-postcard Ireland, all misty and green — which he'd coloured and added to as the years flew past.

We left California as changed people. Brother and sister, knowing that a continent and an ocean would soon separate them again, cried and hugged each other with the awful sense of finality that only such partings can bring. Those three short weeks were a flash of pure joy in their beleaguered lives, like the joining together of a precious vase that had been broken, its shards scattered in separate rooms. They had at last met, had managed to match the motifs and fit together the pieces of their lives, making the patterns merge again into a design of familial love.

When together for that brief time they had lived and laughed and loved every precious minute of every precious day; they were living life as it should be lived, because they feared that there were only so many tomorrows left to them.

That adventure affected me too, adding to the slim sheaf of experiences I carried in my head. When I stepped outside the boundaries of my homeland I became aware of the boundlessness of my own possibilities. There was a wider world out there, surging with life, where people ran and jumped into the gush and swell of things with arms open wide and faces turned towards the sun. There were people of all ages who cried 'yes!' to the universe and took chances, who accepted me for who I was and didn't look for failings. There was a zingy spirituality in California I'd experienced through John Henry; its citizens had locked fear and inhibitions firmly away and replaced them with unconditional acts of kindness, gaiety and love. In California I came close to seeing how wonderful life could be. The experience took away a chunk of fear and replaced it with hope. My abiding memory of America is of a fearless, generous and open people.

I hoped that one day I could live sequestered from the mundane in a foreign land, just as John had done, reinventing myself as I went along, free from the verdicts and reproofs of others, and finding my own way. For the first time I was made aware of the sheer freedom that goes with anonymity. I knew, however, that living abroad for me was nothing more than a hopeless dream. Every time I imagined it the image of my mother came rushing in to quell it, proving that my love for her was stronger than any need I had for independence. Conversely that love she had for me was keeping me bound. So I held my dreams in check and put the exotic picture to one side for one day in the future.

But my spirit, ever mindful of my plight, dealt with my dilemma in the only way it could. One year later, suddenly and without warning, my mother was taken from me. I stumbled, grief-stricken and helpless, to face the enormous void she left behind, the void that only a mother can fill and which from that day forward would for ever remain empty.

> I got up; the chilly sun
> Saw me walk away alone.

FACING THE VOID

I experienced her leave-taking as a sequence out of time. In her absence the world stopped.

Did she see the end coming? I believe she did. In the preceding weeks there had been an air of great sadness about her, as if she were winding down, preparing to go. As though she wanted to. She'd had enough; had flailed her way through the torturous ocean that was her married life. Single-handed she'd loved and nourished us all into the maturing light of adulthood, had fought our battles for us, had stood between our father and us as our protector and champion.

The lines on her hands and face mapped the deepest troughs of that exhausting journey. Her body bore the scars of childbirth and heartache — the heartache she strove to quell by the only means she knew, eating to dull the anguish and drive the pain away.

Seen in hindsight, she appeared to begin her preparations some weeks before. She redecorated a bedroom, the very one where Great-aunt Rose had rattled and banged for our attention a decade earlier. Mother gave the portentous warning that this would be the room that would hold her coffin; when she went she didn't want the neighbours to see an untidy house. We'd laugh and tell her not to be talking nonsense, but she'd just give us a mournful smile and shake her head. It was as if God had let her in on a secret, as if they'd fixed the date and set the time, and she was beginning to feel the act of that epiphany in the quiet of her heart. Her mind was made up and there was no going back.

A month later the secret was out. She died at breakfast while sipping her coffee. The heart she'd told us so often was breaking finally did just that. I was not with her at the time but from all accounts the heart attack was swift and, one hopes, painless. There'd been no struggle or gasping to hold on to life, just a dignified withdrawal, a carrying off on a now-restful sea towards the peace that was hers.

Sleep after toil, port after stormy seas;
Ease after war, death after life does greatly please.

I've often wondered since about the thoughts that must have rushed at her then, battering their wings against the dying light before she moved towards that astonishing calm and a voice that soothed: 'It's time.'

At last a lifetime's invocations had been answered; all that imploring at the gates of heaven with novena books and rosary beads had been rewarded.

I was at a friend's house in Draperstown when I got the phone call. That journey home — on the road I'd travelled so often to school — was the hardest I've ever made. On that cold November morning I found her laid out on the bed in the freshly painted bedroom. All the colour had been leeched from the scene. She looked as still and tranquil as the monochrome image of her wedding picture, with the calmness of the proud bride; the serenity on the face of the lifeless wife and mother held no clue to the drama she had acted out in the interim.

I thought of the last time I had seen her, only the night before, wearing the last clothes she'd ever wear: a green skirt, a navy cardigan, the heavy stockings and suede shoes. She'd half-turned in the doorway to wave to me and beam a smile.

'See you tomorrow then,' she'd said. And with that inauspicious parting she'd walked out of my life. The words of Emily Dickinson come with such clarity of meaning to me now.

> We never know we go when we are going;
> We jest and shut the door.
> Fate — following — behind us bolts it,
> And we accost no more.

When I thought of the warm presence she had been, now reduced to the cold, lifeless figure on the bed, all the love I had for her stirred and stretched and broke in me. I never knew I had so many discordant notes, or so many tears, or points and jabs of pain or questions of 'why'. I had never experienced sorrow of such magnitude and felt certain during its onslaught that I would never experience the like of it again. It was a sliver of comfort amid the anguish, but a comfort none the less, that gave me the faintest, briefest hope. I was undergoing a rite of passage that everyone must go through. No indeed, I would never experience the like of it again; like all mothers she was irreplaceable.

I had not been rehearsed in this part, did not know my lines or moves or how long before my stage cue. It was as though the orchestra had ceased playing, the welcoming applause had subsided and the audience had settled down in the rustling silence; I was left alone on the boards, in the wash of a single spotlight with no one to prompt me or show me what to do.

My mother was no longer there to take my hand and lead me off into the safety of the wings, away from the glare. The hand that had released me at the school gate on that first day had come back and led me home.

The loneliness of those Sunday afternoons of my childhood, while she slept and I played, had always ended with her waking up and restoring me. In all the dramas of my life she'd been there, the alpha and omega of me. But this time she'd gone to sleep for good and I'd never feel her hand in mine again, never see her smile or hear her voice or tumbling laugh or be moved by her tuneless whistle when she stood behind me watching me apply paint to canvas. She was unaware of that whistling but I knew that it was her anthem of appreciation and it always made me smile.

I wailed and cried and kept asking God 'why'. Why take away my caring mother and leave me here alone, leave us all alone, with the heartless father? This swilltub of feeling made me want to race from the house of injury and just keep running; powered by my anger and pain until I got to the edge of the world where I'd launch myself off into the furious stillness and just keep falling, sweeping and diving and falling for ever. Freedom. Oblivion. Bliss.

The sorrow of losing her returned me to childhood — as indeed all deep sorrow does — to the naked, wailing vulnerability of the infant. I remembered all the parts I'd never play again; all the delicious trivialities I'd taken for granted came back to me with the sharpness of a Dürer etching.

I saw myself waiting on the other side of all those changing-room curtains; waiting with my ready praise, zipping her into dresses and helping her on with coats, coaxing her thinning, damp hair into rollers — 'Be careful at the temples; I haven't much left there' — displaying a finished painting and hearing her adulation flow; sharing the binges, sharing the laughs, sharing the silence between the talk, and all the while being close enough to see what little joy she knew in life reflected in her eyes.

The beautiful essence that was her had been spilled and could not be gathered up again. The finality of that separation was appalling. The loneliness she left behind was of an entirely different order, one that thrust me back into nothingness and made me clutch helplessly at invisibles.

> When my silent terror cried,
> Nobody, nobody replied.

The rural Irish deal with death by holding on. For three whole days she lay in that room to be viewed and prayed over by visiting friends and neighbours. The curtains were drawn and the window opened to let her spirit roam free.

Roses and candles 'soothed the bedside'. She lay with a crucifix on her breast and rosary beads entwined in the opalescent fingers, as pure and immutable as the statues of virgins and saints she'd collected and assembled on the sills down the years. I looked at those hands that so often had washed dishes, knitted sweaters, kneaded bread. Hands that were made to clutch and grip and grasp; hands that without work had no meaning; hands that were meaningless now, stilled into serenity at last.

People came with food and muttered condolences, the awkward clichés that surround death. I saw them glide through the darkened house, heard the echoing timbre of their voices.

'She went very quick.'

'She's surely in heaven.'

'She was a great woman altogether, had time for everybody.'

My vibrant mother reduced so soon to a set of past tense verbs! I dearly wished I could be one of those strangers, with no burdens to carry save for their uneasy words of solace while I sat crushed under the weight of mine.

She was buried on the stark crispness of a winter's morning. The world had been pared back to its fictive bones, stripped and scrubbed bare of all meaning, a metaphor for my sorrow. The pale sun hung like a communion host in a Canaletto sky; ravens cawed and squawked at the invasion in the graveyard. I can still hear their raw refrain desecrating the silence. I can still feel the numbness of each modulated action of that morning; the weight of her coffin on my right shoulder, the unwilling legs that stumbled over the cold-stiffened soil towards the gaping wound of earth that was her grave, the sinking farewell of those nine roses that were scattered down upon her, our final acts of love before the heartless thud of stones and earth upon timber. Perhaps it was that last which upset me most that morning. The thudding upon the coffin lid; a most inelegant conclusion to her life.

The desolation she left in her wake was measured by the depth of our sorrow. The days and weeks and months could do nothing to assuage it. And, oh dear — how my father wept — all the unused love coming out in splashing tears. His servant had died. Who would 'do for him' now? Who would fill the famished hours with the endless cups of tea, the meals that were never right?

I'd sit in the bedroom that had held her coffin and hope vainly to hear her tapping for my attention, just as old Rose had done. But in my heart I knew it was pointless. Her goodness in life, her compassion and suffering were the prayers that gave her rest in eternity. She had no need to ask for our help. She wasn't coming back.

For weeks afterwards the biggest regret I carried was that I had never hugged her or told her that I loved her and for the first time I understood the potency of the dictum which says that when we lose someone we love, our bitterest tears are called forth by the memory of hours when we did not love enough.

My mother had not been in the habit of demonstrating her love with embraces. We lived in a kind of reciprocal alliance; my paintings were my tokens of love towards her, her admiration of them was hers.

Such inhibition is a feature of the 'Irish way', so I took my cues from her. This shared shyness had made us incapable of expressing that most fundamental of desires. Each night I cried myself to sleep with the frustration of that neglect rioting through me. Why could I not have performed such a simple act? Why was the language of love so difficult to express? And now it was too late.

But she heard my plea and came to me in a dream one night, quietly smiling, and gave me the biggest and longest hug I could ever have wished for; its strength melted away all the dereliction I felt inside. She was happy at last. I got up the next morning elated and healed. She'd come in the night at the sound of my cries and wiped all my tears away. Still the loving, dutiful mother, stepping over from that other world to take care of me in this one.

Offering it Up

My life changed from that point onward. I realised that the coherent narrative I'd assigned to it had been altered beyond measure. My mother's untimely death had warped the fundamental meaning of all I held dear. There had been no happy ending for her, no fanfares of applause or awards of recognition for her endeavour. She had lived and suffered the life a repressive rural society had moulded for its benefit but at her expense, and she died with all the injustice of it in her heart.

Her own mother had been her sole example. It also followed that, with an inadequate education and no access to books, the acquisition of a husband — preferably a wealthy one — became the future prize she had to win. She had two attributes that gave her a head start in the race to attract a mate: she was slim and she was beautiful. It was ironic and cruel; the two factors that assured the near-certainty of marriage would swiftly be consumed and destroyed by marriage itself.

The slim beauty met her handsome prince. The wedding picture is a potent reminder.

> How beautiful you were, and near, and young,
> So vivid, you might still be there among
> Those first few days, unfingermarked again.

Their courtship was brief and father played the chivalrous suitor convincingly, reverting to form once the vows had been exchanged and the bride had been ringed and requisitioned.

I wonder at what point she realised her mistake; was it as he rushed ahead of her down Grafton Street after the photo session, or in Bewley's café when he thumped the chair with such alarming disapproval? The short answer is probably 'yes, both'; knowing so little then, she dismissed those ungracious actions as shortcomings that could be worked on and changed. But as time passed she must have perceived the awful reality that lay beneath that which she'd placed her hope and trust in.

The peaceful life she'd wanted and envisaged that day in the café remained, but the cherished snapshot of fantasy — the peace and freedom that picture offered — hung for ever in the useless distance. All her life she strained towards it like a drowning soul for a branch, her fingers never quite grasping the hold that would pull her free.

Each year of the first ten years of her marriage a baby appeared, yelling and screaming for the love and attention only she was prepared to give it. Each successive birth heaped yet more burden upon her suffering. We children did not bring her joy, we simply added to her pain and the torment of her unfulfilled self.

Germaine Greer insists that motherhood is a never-ending condition, and that bearing children causes a woman to suffer more pain than she could ever have imagined. Her children, she says, will always cause her pain because they are of far more importance to her than she is to them.

In my mother's case that pain was multiplied by ten not nine, if one counts the ninth child who died aged seven months. She had very little choice available to her when that gold wedding band was slipped onto her finger; in fact she forfeited her right to freedom by her acceptance of it. My father caused her more pain than all nine of us put together. Only by changing the circumstances that were causing such anguish could she be liberated from her sorrow, and she could not change the circumstances because society had rendered her powerless.

Women of her era had no choice but to remain captives. She had neither job nor money of her own to enable her to make more life-affirming choices. She grew up with a trenchant adherence to Luther's axiom that a woman's place is in the home and with the Church's unyielding stance regarding the sanctity of marriage, and its inviolability, no matter what the situation.

The law in those times did not favour disaffected wives, and this injustice was to endure up until recently, when finally the courage of the Women's Movement shone a torchlight in the guilty face of Ireland's blatant oppression. In rural Ireland we saw little of the feminist revolution that swept through Western society in the 1960s. The Church and the menfolk were having none of it.

I understand now much of what moved my mother then. When she shouted at us children and cried and raged so frequently, she was transmuting all that frustration and sadness into the anguished phrases she knew would hurt us too. Christ was never off duty when mother was around: whether in oath or prayer she blasted out the Holy name with all the force she could muster, flooring us with those frequent rants about the sorry state of her life.

The tragedy is that she had no other means of expressing her despair; offloading it onto us made her feel somewhat relieved and lighter. We helped her carry her cross; we, the unfortunate innocents caught in the nuptial crossfire.

As a child I hated to see my mother cry. Sometimes she'd take a walk to a distant field, just to get away from us, to steal a glimmer of peace in the solitude of a meadow. I would stumble after her, unnoticed, making my small, determined way over the ruts of the baked earth, falling down to dirty my knees and skirting puddles just to see where she was going. I'd always find her in the same place, sitting on a fallen tree, silently weeping, and I would weep too. She would get up then, dry my tears, tenderly take my hand and lead me home.

We suffered along with her solely because my father refused to unlock the love that was in him, share it and so set us free. She knew she was fighting a losing battle. Marrying had not only cancelled out her name, it left her dreams of love and peace unfulfilled.

The Catholic Church, mother's great succour, could not entertain the thought of an unhappy marriage. If her religion taught her anything then it taught her the language of repression.

The Church was clear on the woman's role. Women were to serve, obey and produce babies; love hardly got a look in. 'Offer it up' and 'This is the cross you have to bear' were phrases I heard often when I was growing up. So many women of my mother's generation took those platitudes as the dogma of their deliverance, and struggled to make sense of it all through a constant round of novenas, masses and rosaries.

Some might regard the Catholic Church as an easy target, yet surely it deserves our criticism. This Christian organisation has flourished for centuries on the anguished silence of women like my mother, and the onerous chauvinism that drives it remains in place. This unwillingness to acknowledge the debt that is owed is realised in its insistence on a male-only priesthood.

How different things might have been. Jesus and Paul viewed men and women as equal partners, to enjoy equality and mutual respect. However things had changed by the time the later scriptures came to be written. Misogyny and the fear of sex are evident, particularly in the post-Pauline 'Letter to the Ephesians':

> Wives, submit yourselves unto your own husbands, as unto the Lord. For the husband is the head of the wife, even as Christ is the head of the Church: and he is the saviour of the body. Therefore as the Church is subject unto Christ, so let the wives be to their own husbands in everything. ...

Taken together these attitudes and restrictions contributed to the unhappy circumstances in which my mother found herself. Her pain and grief were those of the caged bird, yet she felt them far more keenly than a feathered creature could.

This was her cruel reality. She died with the gathering awareness that she'd served her time; all the years of pain had been 'offered up' over and over again. Paradise surely awaited her. She embraced death; she did not fear it. Her unhappiness had brought her to this pass.

Roll-call of Death

Father survived her by 19 years. With the exception of James, each of the McKenna brothers made his world-weary exit before him. James and father died within hours of each other, battling it out with the Grim Reaper one sunless afternoon in August 1999, defiantly clinging on to the end. I would like to be able to say that after mother's death my father had softened in the light of the cruel reality that the loss of a loved one brings. That simply was not the case. He carried on as if nothing had happened, the absent father who made his presence felt through indifference and contempt. He expected his daughters to become the substitute servants and for a time we rallied round as best we could. But we had jobs and other responsibilities. Times had changed and father hadn't noticed.

Towards the end of his life I looked in vain for a sign that would acknowledge our pain, something that would serve to lift the inestimable weight of suffering he'd caused in all our lives. But sadly, in all his remaining days, his 'mind lay open like a drawer of knives'.

The little love he'd allowed himself to experience went towards the carpentry he had by turns admired and attacked in public, and tried to emulate in private. As a child I would hear the bitter music of hammer and saw in the toolshed which was his domain. In there he was doing what he did best: driving home the nails, making that wood outdo itself with the chairs and shelves he would carry into the house.

He had built the house we'd been raised in brick by brick and had left the imprint of his hands on window frames and doors. The scrubbed table in the kitchen — rock-steady and functional — spoke of the life he'd always wanted. The life of the woodworker, before his wife and children had got in the way.

I can still hear the disenchantment in his voice, like the rasp of an unoiled hinge.

I can still see him in the fields, bent and wordless over a shovel, slicing into tubers, sinking all that anger and regret deep into the soil. The injustice that he felt was never of *his* making; it was we, his family, who'd snatched his dream away.

When I wept at my father's graveside I shed tears that were not of sorrow for the father I would miss, but rather tears of sadness for the father he could have been.

It was otherwise with Uncle Robert, the schoolmaster, keeper of the family fortune. Robert, in whose lifetime pleasure sank and hardship rose, who was always careful never to get carried away on the crest of things. He made a sudden exit one morning after his daily jaunt to Draperstown. Edward found him in the musty parlour, slumped at his desk, with the *Irish News* spread out before him, opened, significantly, at the obituaries column.

The millionaire died in his grey raincoat in a house without electricity or running water. His final view was through a grimy window overlooking the yard where sat his one extravagance: the Ford Anglia. In the bank sat the fortune he'd amassed and guarded throughout his adult life, swelling with the interest Robert would never enjoy.

And James? James was paralysed by a stroke. All that movement of arm-flapping and indecision was arrested on a chilly day, the thirteenth day of November, on the thirteenth anniversary of my mother's death. James, who had grasped the meaning of land and money but never the meaning of life, endured a stalled existence in a disconnected world for the final eight years of his life. Like father, he remained steadfastly unrepentant to the end.

Edward, the occasional drinker, the underdog, had the happiest departure of all. He smiled and called for his harmonica to serenade himself into eternity.

It could be said that each of the brothers had died at 25 and was buried between the ages of 70 and 83. They spent their lives preparing for life instead of living it, and each left the planet never having known the meaning of love and happiness.

My uncles Dan and John by contrast died in the midst of 'living', John Henry after completing another hectic day at the *Sacramento Bee*, Dan while engaged in the humble task of bringing in fuel for the fire.

They all went in time, those people of Ballinascreen who had populated and shaped my childhood, the gentle and the vain. Down the funnel of time I can see 'Aunt' Margaret sitting in a tweed chair by a hospital bed. Her stomach swollen with cancer. Margaret — nearing the end of a life sprung from loneliness and longing, who'd never heard the music that had beckoned her to dance — wearing that same distracted look, still questing for answers, still wondering what it was all about. The urge to hug her was strong, to let her know that she'd always belonged, but I knew that such an alien gesture would confirm for her what she didn't want to know. That she indeed was dying. So for her sake I tearfully turned away, taking with me the Judas kiss and the last embrace that would have both delivered and betrayed me.

My mother's true and dear friend Helen died five years after mother's passing. She was 52, too young and too good to have gone so early. She took with her a reservoir of my mother's confidences, audaciously purified throughout all their years of friendship. With her going she broke the final link that held me to my mother but in her wake left such beautiful recollections that forever stir and caress my memory, like remnants of silk in a breeze.

Both my primary schoolteachers, the unassuming Miss McKeague and the unpredictable Master Bradley, took very different routes into that everlasting light. Miss died happily and peacefully as she slept, and the Master by his own hand.

In retrospect the Master's manner of exit should not have surprised us. One September morning, shortly after I'd left Lisnamuck school, he decided he'd had enough and drove many miles up the Antrim coast to the Giant's Causeway. He did not, however, stop at this much frequented beauty spot but continued for seven more miles along the coast until he arrived at Carrick-a-Rede rope bridge. Every year the local salmon fishermen sling this precarious bridge across the 60-foot wide and 80-foot deep chasm that separates the mainland from the islet of Carrick-a-Rede. But Master Bradley had not come to admire the scenery on that fateful morning. He stepped out onto the bridge, ventured halfway across, and flung himself off into the surging breakers.

I attended his funeral and stood with other past-pupils at the graveside. There were no tears. As his coffin was lowered I was aware that some kind of blemished justice had come to my classmates and me, and to every trembling child who'd sat before him down all the years. A class full of children had waited for his arrival on the morning of his suicide and I could not help thinking of them. They'd waited and prayed with Miss on that sunny

September morning — just as I had done so many times. Were they, I wondered, struck by a bolt of pure joy on learning that they'd never see him again? An era of suffering had ended, because Master Bradley had decided to kill the suffering within himself.

From Fear to Love

Though I did not know it at the time, those who made me suffer were in far greater pain than I was. As I grew up I began to realise that there was a valuable lesson to be learned: I saw how negativity garnered nothing but unhappiness in a person's life, and this made me want to look for more positive alternatives. I was beginning to see that by understanding the *meaning* behind the chaos I could learn from it, rather than repeat the same negative patterns. I began to see that it is not the events of our lives that shape us but our understanding of what those events signify.

My father, like his brothers, was totally opposed to change. Had our mother not been there to cajole him then life would have been unbearable. There'd have been no birthday cards or Christmas presents, and no annual day trip to Portstewart. These snatches of happiness rescued us; it was *her* love that gave us hope.

Father lived his entire life looking to the past — never mind that this past was a far from happy one. The old ways were the only ways he allowed to guide him, and therefore were the 'best' in his opinion. So opposed to change was he that he'd 'taken on the job of stopping the world'. This fixed reality, quite naturally, never brought him happiness. It brings happiness to nobody.

Beliefs can be either empowering or destructive. We choose the tenets which matter to us and live according to them. My father and his family adhered to a set of limiting beliefs about the world; it was as though they were swallowing a small amount of poison every day, until finally they'd ingested so many toxins that the build-up was fatal. With each unquestioned negative their spirits died a little more.

> Courage unused, diminishes,
> Commitment, unexercised waves.
> Love unshared dissipates.

With my father there was little growth or evolution; since we use our minds to evolve it follows that a closed mind cannot do so.

It was the simple, basic, rural pastimes that shaped his life: playing those IRA songs on that green record-player, listening to GAA matches on the wireless and scanning the *Sunday Press* before falling asleep on a Sunday afternoon. He farmed the land according to the monotonous dictates of the calendar and expressed himself within confines of his own making. Such unchanging activities and circumstances could hardly produce creative thought. To change is to grow; the more varied our experiences, the more knowledge we accumulate about ourselves and the world.

Even from an early age I suspected there was something very skewed about the way he looked at life. His conversations usually started out with bland comments on the weather or the farm and ended with the defamation of someone's character. No one was ever good enough — for the simple reason that he did not feel he himself was good enough. When we're unhappy with ourselves, when we are fearful, we perceive others as flawed. It is easier to judge them than to look at ourselves objectively, and perhaps make the necessary adjustments. It was impossible to escape the fallout from this warped thinking. I grew up believing that to be critical and judgemental of others was the norm. I absorbed all this negativity and became a fearful child and for many years an unhappy adult.

It is a terrible indictment of the human animal that when a person of low self-esteem is given power over another his first thoughts turn to how he can set about torturing that other. History proves this time and again. My father had no power in his life until he married and had children. Being himself the product of a loveless marriage, he felt that the only way to deal with the awfulness of those early years, and 'right' the wrongs done to him, was to repeat the same pattern with us. He withheld love from us in order that we might experience the pain of his childhood. This prolonged act of vengeance never brought him happiness, however.

We children were his opportunity to experience the love he'd been denied. Ignoring this fact simply created more resistance in his life. He had nine offspring and several decades to figure out what it was he was doing wrong. It saddens me that he died never having experienced all the love that was there for the giving and receiving. Love is our greatest miracle. To love unselfishly surely is our highest calling; it's our only antidote to fear, and with this recognition comes understanding, tolerance, open-mindedness and peace.

I wish that he and his brothers could have come to this realisation, this appreciation of the essence of life. Sadly they did not. Life was something that happened to others while they sat contemplating the land and money that would one day be theirs. When the oldest of them, Robert, died and the golden prize was in sight, all the happiness they'd postponed since youth did not suddenly erupt like struck oil into their lives. By the time it arrived they were too old and embittered; the long wait had made them so. Whatever illusions they might have had as young men lay collapsed and broken like the decaying barns in the yard, the nettles and briars of those neglected dreams growing up to choke out the light.

People do not grow old, someone once remarked; when they cease to grow they become old.

Along with those limited belief systems I also received religion of a sort. In my youth I witnessed a dedication to the Church which, seen at close quarters, turned out to be hypocrisy. It served to distance me from churchgoers in general as I gained control of my own life. Christian teaching did not seem to figure much in the day-to-day lives of those around me; I suspected that prayer was otherwise than the empty words I encountered during the celebration of the sacraments. There were definite echoes of Shakespeare's King Claudius:

> My words go up, my thoughts remain below.
> Words without thoughts never to heaven go.

I saw also that the nature of God was open to all sorts of misinterpretation. That supernatural event following my great-aunt's death had proved to me not only the existence of a supreme being but also the reality of a parallel and invisible universe where the dead lived on in spirit.

I watched as mass and confession were attended on a regular basis, sins were forgiven and communion received; I saw a 'huge remembering' of the importance of God for a half-hour on a Sunday or when someone died – 'God, it's too bad wee Barney's gone ... suppose it comes to us all' – then it would be back to the anger and resentment, the scheming and prejudging.

On most evenings there'd be my mother's order: 'All down on your knees for the rosary this minute.' And on each occasion my mind was duly numbed by the rambling decades of petitioning prayers. I prayed without conviction because the idea of God sold to me as a child was an abstract one I could neither relate to nor understand. I gained little solace from weekly attendance at mass and the fortnightly visits to the confessional. Those sacraments only served to induce great fear and give me an exaggerated sense of my own inferiority. If believing in a god was supposed to make me a better person then why did I not *feel* better, why was I not experiencing all the 'love and peace' that were on offer?

I could see that my mother, for all her devotion, was not experiencing any of this love or peace either, so I could not learn it from her. The guardians of our morality — the priests and bishops — inhabited an elevated region that was so far above us laity that we felt we could never hope to breathe their rarified, incense-rich air. Miss McKeague, with all her well-intentioned pious wisdom, could not explain to me that I was 'God's success story'. Are not all of us worthy of this description, regardless of colour, creed or class? No one told me that this was so.

Every year the 'stations' were performed in our home; mass was said by the local priest and the neighbours were invited to participate. The ceremony was rotated to ensure that the home of each family in the parish was thus honoured. In the wake of Great-aunt Rose's haunting, our back bedroom became the place of celebration.

The stations were conducted in early morning. I remember the tremendous effort my mother put into the preparations, akin to those preparations for the Yankees but with infinitely less colour and flounce attached. The best linen was taken out and she'd worry for weeks in advance about the priest's breakfast. A humble egg was treated like the most exotic delicacy. Mother would try to second-guess the priest's preferences: would he want it boiled, fried, scrambled or poached? All eating utensils, polished to perfection, lay in readiness in the kitchen. And oh, how that table sparkled! The china gleamed, the silver shone, the butter 'curled' and marmalade glittered in a crystal dish: a table fit for a king. And invariably the priest would spoil it all by announcing that he'd like, 'a slice or two of toast and nothing else, thanks'.

In my young head the priest was an all-powerful being who had been heaven-sent to our humble home to keep us all from the raging fires of hell. My parents' deference and the obsequious silence that prevailed in his presence told me that he was the most important person in the parish and beyond. The clergy of that era willingly colluded in this burlesque. Such barriers and condescension did not lead to understanding or further the Christian teachings of humility. My catechism taught me that we were all 'one in the sight of God'; the practice told me different.

It took me a considerable time to understand why religion and reality can sometimes be at odds. Wresting the truth from the wreckage involved dismantling piece by piece the scaffolding that had held in place all the chaotic beliefs I'd grown up with. I have since discovered that the reason for the dissonance between man and God lies primarily in *man's* interpretation of what God is.

The journey towards 'understanding' this anomaly started at my mother's graveside. I travelled through the years and countless books that might render up the answer. I took John Henry's lead, wanted to experience the fearless, careless beauty of a life such as his, and went to live and work abroad. I travelled, taught and painted in foreign lands for ten years, soaring back and forth across the skies, shuffling exotic coinage in my pocket, balancing alien languages on my tongue, and discovering to my amazement that all of those countries with all of their problems and delights held the same people — often fearful, sometimes loving — all of them presenting the same emotions as myself.

And all those experiences, and all those people, all of the obstacles and triumphs I encountered in my search, moved me towards the beauty of one truth; moved me ineluctably towards the 'undeniable beauty of the one and only truth' — that love is our only reality and that God is love.

There are only two emotions: love and fear. Love is God-given; it is our natural state. Fear is what we experience when we refuse to love.

When we refuse to love, the fear we feel condemns us to live in a hell of our own making. We express this fear through all the negative emotions: anger, greed, selfishness, violence. We become anxious, depressed, lonely and sad. In short, fear is our protest against the reality of what we truly are.

However the hard part is that in order to experience love in our own lives we must give love to others, not just family and friends — that's easy — but to strangers, people we perceive to be different, whether because of their skin colour or their religion; or because they don't have as much money as we do. It means that the beggar in the street, the struggling single mother, the 'special' child, the disabled adult, the lonely but cantankerous pensioner all deserve our love and respect because we are all equal parts of the human family.

To give love to another is to strengthen it in ourselves; to withhold it diminishes love in ourselves. Hence the meaning of the axiom: It is in giving that we receive.

The founders of every major religion — be they Jesus, Buddha or Mohammed — have all taught the doctrine of loving one's neighbour. Therefore there is only one religion, the religion of love. Such an understanding renders all other labels superfluous.

All the conflict in the world today demonstrates our shared lovelessness, dating back to childhoods that were marred by one parent or another's unwillingness to give love. Lack of love in the home leads to lack of peace in the world. Northern Ireland is one crude example.

No one in Ulster who ever planted a bomb, fired a stone, bullet or volley of invective at another adult or child did so out of a sense of patriotism. Rather their motives stemmed from the feeling that they were unloved, and therefore felt unworthy. When we feel 'bad' about ourselves we want to hurt others so that they can feel our pain as well. Every act of violence is a call for love. But hurting others will not ease our pain. Hurting others will not give us back the love we yearn for. Only loving and forgiving will get us there.

Reclaiming the love that was denied me in childhood, understanding why it was withheld, and forgiving those people who refused to love and support me enables me to stop the blame game and so right the wrongs of the past.

My Catholic upbringing taught me a great deal about sin and guilt but failed to emphasise the essential premise that all answers lie within. I looked for God everywhere: up in the sky, inside chapels and great cathedrals, and in the stones of those painful penitential beds on Lough

Derg. I could not locate Him anywhere. And all the while He sat patiently in my heart, waiting to be acknowledged, the dweller within us all. I was never told that the surest way to hear Him was not necessarily through prayer but through meditation and silence.

In the light of what I've learned I can forgive all those unkind adults from my past — the uncles who never once showed they cared, the teachers who yelled, the master who beat me, those people who threw their rocks and stones before me and watched me fall. But most importantly of all I can forgive my poor father: he with his resistance to change, his unwillingness to love, his ignorance of the splendour life could hold. He, who more than anyone else bent and buckled my childhood out of shape and pushed me towards an adulthood of shattered hopes and angst-ridden longings.

I can forgive him because I now see that he blindly followed the script his fearful parents had passed unto him, the one they had accepted without question from *their* parents; an entire three-act play of fear. The words 'act' and 'fear' belong together in this context, because when we live in fear we are really acting a part. In *A Course in Miracles*, undoubtedly the definitive work on enlightenment, it states:

> Only perfect love exists
> If there is fear,
> It produces a state that does not exist.

As a child I read from this script of fear because as a child I had no choice. However when I reached adulthood I did have a choice. The script was a damaged one which did not make me happy. It was based on fear and produced a life of unworkable realities. So I tore it up and began to write my own and in doing so I discovered that the only way to transcend that fearful past was to understand it and so forgive it.

To hold any resentment would mean that I was simply repeating my father's pattern; it would mean that I was making the choice to live in ignorance. Were I to make that choice then my spirit would shrivel up and die, as surely as the sun rises and sets.

I truly believe that all things in life are 'lessons that God would have us learn' and that my father's life is the lesson that God would have me learn *from*. I do not pretend to know how astrophysics works, yet my ignorance does not affect our galaxy in any way; however if I do not question the reality of my own self then how can I ever expect to progress and learn and so become a better human being?

Every time I make a negative statement or judgement it's my father's voice I hear. In giving in to his voice I realise that I forfeit the spiritual in me; that I shrink to fit a *lesser* me and give voice to the fearful me. I must always be on guard. This awareness is pivotal to my spiritual growth.

And finally, all those years ago when I experienced the supernatural in the boys' bedroom and embraced language and colour in the classroom, two new worlds came into being for me — the spirit world and the spiritual experience.

From the haunting I learned that when we choose to live a loveless life, this unnatural choice can actually have repercussions in the parallel world of spirit when we transfer to that dimension.

When I started to paint and write I understood that it was really a collaboration between myself and my higher self. The more I left things in the hands of that divine part of me the more successful the result.

And it is the same with life. The more I choose love over fear, or God over the ego, the happier I become.

I can now appreciate the fine people who sustained me and gave me hope, the few shining examples I found along the way: those whose positive example lifted me up and carried me forward. I had my mother's love, Helen's kindness, my first teacher's goodness, Uncle Dan's humility, John Henry's drive, the praise of those teachers in the English and art lessons and, in the creative stillness, the artistic vision of Kandinsky and the flawless verse of Heaney, Larkin and MacNeice.

Ultimately I've discovered that we must take the negative experiences from our lives and learn from them, and that the positive experiences, even though they may be few and far between, are there for us to build on.

> Where there is no vision the people perish.
> Proverbs 29:18

A scene enacts itself now in my mind's eye. It's a vision that refuses to be ignored.

I stand alone and unnoticed, a stranger in an unknown land. In a far-off field there is a party in progress. The sun shines brightly on this blithe spot, making it shimmer and glow with such vibrancy that the surrounding countryside recedes into the shadow.

The guests at the picnic seem very happy. I hear their laughter and talk and they are like streams of evanescent song carried to me on the breeze. Everything is effortless; people link arms and join hands as if they've been friends for eons. There are no inhibitions here, or neglect or loneliness. There is harmony and inclusion, and feelings of kinship and love. These feelings are so strong that they create their own force field — I feel it radiating outward and it has the power to touch me even at a distance.

The guests are well known to me. There is my mother – I focus on her first; she shines in her yellow dress and is smiling and talking to a gent in a nautical outfit. Those flashes of red cravat and hankie could only belong to one man: my effervescent Uncle John. Lying on the grass I see Sam, propped up on an elbow, chatting to his neighbour Helen, who suddenly twirls on those white stilettos of hers, and laughs.

Mr Edward Bradley has just arrived. He's parked his motorcycle under a nearby tree and is struggling out of his leathers. And what is that he's extracting from his satchel? It's a fish, a salmon plucked from the great Moyola river, at last. Beside his motorcycle I see that great bicycle of Mary Catherine's, still hung with the red-and-grey spangled shopping bag, full of brandy balls and novenas. She is in deep conversation with my angelic first teacher, Miss McKeague.

My favourite teacher is forever her smiling, attentive self; the brooch and the watch with its anchored handkerchief are still her only adornment, answering to some quiet need in eternity. Beside her there is a lady cutting a jam sponge and surreptitiously sipping sweet sherry. Yes, it could only be dear Margaret. I recognise at once that shiny, thick hair and those unmistakable suede shoes. And who is that in a furious orange inferno of a dress, that brassy wig of curls and straw hat beside him on the grass? It's Norrie, free at last from censure and exclusion.

My Uncle Dan sees me and raises his cap and his hand in greeting; as he does so, the entire assembly turn in my direction to do the same. They open up like a beautiful peacock fan, before folding again and returning to the picnic.

But there are others. I hadn't noticed them before, loitering as they do at a distance from the group. They huddle in sombre clothes, looking sad and forlorn. As I draw closer I see that it's my father and his brothers and my Great-aunt Rose. The vibrant party hasn't escaped their notice — and comment.

The schoolmaster's voice is the loudest. I hear it first.

'I s'pose a body would need tae make a shape over there, on account of Big Frenkie,' he says.

'Not much odds about him,' father answers, and Great-aunt Rose nods in agreement.

But here is Edward, breaking free of the group.

'Don't ye want tae see Mary?' he says. 'She's over there and she's waitin' for ye. She's waitin' for all of us.'

Father responds with his customary dalliance.

'Ah, it's time enough,' he grumbles. 'There's no hurry, so there isn't.'

Uncle James agrees.

But Robert is not so certain and shakes his head.

'Wouldn't be too sure about that!' he says darkly. 'A body can wait too long, you know. I wouldn't want tae end up like that great-uncle of Johnny the Digger's. He waited so long in the same spot that he died; never got livin' atall, atall.' He shakes his head ruefully and adds: 'Aye, and it was on this very spot where it happened, so they say, in eighteen and fifty-six.'

There's a minatory silence while they all consider the Master's words. Edward, however, seems to have made up his own mind; he begins to walk away, in the direction of the party.

Bathed in glorious sunlight, the party continues, joy and happiness abound. Outside the magic circle, fear and loneliness prevail. As I look on the scene I see to my delight that the outsiders are beginning to move — hesitantly at first — but they are moving all the same, in the right direction, towards the party, towards the light. The only thing that will get them there is a willingness to love, a willingness to forgive. A simple lesson that can take a whole lifetime, or many lifetimes, to learn.

Yet of one thing I'm certain. They *will* make it to that party, no matter how long it takes — because God wills it. The miracle of unconditional love is freely available to each and every one of us. That is our purpose here: to discover this great truth for ourselves.

> Each of us inevitable,
> Each of us limitless,
> Each of us with his or her right
> Upon the earth;
> Each of us allow'd
> The eternal purports of the earth;
> Each of us here
> As divinely as any is here.
> Walt Whitman